Reluctant
Neighbors

Reluctant
Neighbors

E. R. BRAITHWAITE

OPEN ROAD

INTEGRATED MEDIA
NEW YORK

Copyright © 1972 by E. R. Braithwaite

Cover design by Mauricio Díaz

ISBN 978-1-4804-5770-6

This edition published in 2014 by Open Road Integrated Media, Inc.
345 Hudson Street
New York, NY 10014
www.openroadmedia.com

For Francis,

    with love and hope

Reluctant
Neighbors

I HAD IT CUT VERY fine, allowing myself barely ten minutes for the half-mile drive from home to the railway station. Two traffic lights and a policeman on duty at the main intersection kept me careful of the 23-m.p.h. limit, but I made it, just beating a white Cadillac to an empty parking meter, my luck continuing with an empty double seat in a fast-filling train compartment. I put my briefcase on the luggage rack and settled myself comfortably near the window, smiling at the memory of the Cadillac driver's furious face, wondering if he'd find another parking space in time to make this train; not much noblesse in the daily hustle by too many cars for too few parking meters in the station forecourt.

I watched the latecomers jostling each other through the doorways, hurrying for the remaining seats, greeting friends and acquaintances, fitting overcoats, briefcases, hats and packages onto the luggage racks and settling down with *The New York Times* or *Wall Street Journal*. Mostly the *Journal*, folded casually, suggesting familiarity with its complexities, as if high finance were the prevailing occupation or ambition, or at least a respectable false front for humbler pursuits. Soon the compartment was full, except for the vacant aisle seat beside me. Hopefuls would rush towards it, then veer away down the aisle and out to another compartment, reminding me of wide-winged bats in the Venezuelan twilight darting narrowly past near-invisible telephone wires. It amused me to observe these travelers and speculate about their acute sensitivity to the invisible presence on the seat beside me, or perhaps to both of us, me and my invisible companion. It had to be him who was frightening them away because, if familiar indicators could be believed, any of them would welcome the company of a successful author-diplomat-educator on the hour-long ride. After all, any normal American is drawn towards titles, position and success.

At last a bolder spirit, who first did the familiar ritual dance up and down the aisle looking for some other seat. Finding none and resignedly broaching the repellent shield around the invisible presence. Sitting on it, settling comfortably on it and carefully putting up his own *Wall Street Journal* barricade. Enough pages to insulate and isolate him all the way to New York. I simply closed my eyes. Then we were off, and immediately we were thrown heavily against each other as if the irreverent train didn't give a damn. Closer than groupies in a sensitivity session. Getting more for our money than our tickets promised. Jammed closer than neighbors with each shuddering jolt, each prolonged sway. After one particularly violent bump I opened my eyes.

My reluctant neighbor was carefully folding his paper in capitulation. Lowering the barricade. I smiled inside myself, anticipating the next move, wondering what he'd use for an opening gambit.

The weather? The war in Vietnam? The so-called Attica rebellion? Stocks? Bonds? Perhaps I could put on an act for him. Wait for the conversational overture, then reply in French or Spanish, or maybe pidgin English. No, that would be too easy. For an occasion like this I needed something exotic. Senegalese or Swahili. Exotic or terribly, terribly strange. But no. He placed the folded newspaper behind him, inched himself forward for greater comfort, closed his eyes and seemed all set to doze through the rest of the journey. The train swayed around a bend and threw him heavily against me.

"Sorry," he apologized, "hope you don't bruise easily."

"Not to worry. I'll survive." Smiling inside myself at how easily I had been trapped into a simple, familiar rejoinder.

"Don't be too sure, my friend. I've been riding this railroad for eighteen years, and I wouldn't take any bets on surviving, believe me." Getting no response, waiting for none. Very knowledgeable about lousy trains, lousy outdated equipment, lousy incompetent management, lousy schedules; the train doing its best to encourage the gentle intrusion.

I thought of the casual "my friend." With that for starters we'd soon be well away now that he'd conceded my presence. But why should I acknowledge his? No, I didn't bruise easily, and even if I did, it wouldn't show. So I could close my eyes again and accept the bumps for the rest of the way.

"Visiting these parts?" His face turned towards me, pink, smooth and narrow, light reflecting off the rimless glasses to obscure the eyes; gray-streaked brown hair worn fashionably long, youthfully uneven. Why the hell would he so readily assume I was visiting these parts? He and I had boarded the same train at the same station which was the departure point for this run into New York. I'd not exchanged more than three or four words with him.

Was there something unusual or unfamiliar about me? Hell, let's play along and see where it might lead.

"No. Residing in these parts." Flat-voiced.

"New Canaan?" The two words hanging there between us, weighted with his surprise, or shock or unbelief.

"Yes. New Canaan. Why?" My guts tightening.

"No reason. Just that I make this run daily and I'd not seen you before." Trailing it off, backing away from whatever it was he heard in my voice. If he'd been lucky enough to find another seat his record for not seeing me would have remained unbroken. The way he'd said "New Canaan?" Nose, mouth, spectacles, everything about him sharing in the surprise, the shock, that an outsider had invaded his sovereign earth. I swallowed to ease the dryness in my throat, the hot rage mushrooming inside me. Arbitrarily, contemptuously they believed themselves entitled to the best on no other qualification than that pallid skin. 1971, and nothing had really changed. Zoning laws had replaced the NIGGER KEEP OUT signs, but hell, those stately trees could still support a weighted rope.

Steady, I advised myself. Keep it cool. So it happened today a little earlier than yesterday. But it was sure to happen. The time, the place, the manner of its happening was of little consequence. Sometime in the course of each day, or that part of each day that I spend in inevitable intercourse with the white man, his contempt will seek some way of expressing itself. Each day. Every day. And me, stupid me, always so preoccupied with simple concerns of living and doing, and always caught unprepared for the indignity and the contempt. Today was no exception. This son-of-a-bitch beside me.

Cool it, man. Again I told myself. Control, man. Turning to look at him. It was there, the contempt a ubiquitous nuance in his every word, an irritating dimension to his every look, a broken thread in the uncertain fabric of his smile.

"Do you live in New Canaan?" I asked him. Not caring. Not really wanting to know.

"Oh, yes. All my life. Born and raised here . . . " ready to let it flow, but I cut it short.

"That's rather strange. It just occurred to me that I'd never seen you around before." Unsmiling.

He hesitated, as if pondering that, then: "Touché." He laughed, holding both arms up in mock surrender, a risky venture on that roller-coaster train. The stone in his college ring fleetingly caught and held a glint of sunlight. "I walked right into that one, didn't I?" Chuckling and straightening himself, adjusting the position of his body towards me. Legs crossed carefully to preserve the sharp crease in the slacks of his green-flecked brown suit. Making the chameleon change. Ready for conversation. Seeing only my pin-striped gray suit and black face. He couldn't know about the rage which could overspill at any moment. That bit about New Canaan was jangling discordantly in my ear. What the hell was so special about New Canaan? The air was clean. Sure. Green trees every-where, park land and garbage-free streets. Sure. And courteous policemen, friendly shop assistants and the welcome wagon. Side-walks free of the dog-shit hazard. Fine. But the people, black and white, all wore one head on one body with two arms and legs and occasionally bad complexions. Like everywhere else. And the rents were high. Not a damned thing was for free. Not the clean air or the green trees, or the skunks doing their nightly thing under my bedroom window.

"What's your field?" his voice intruded on my musing.

"I beg your pardon?"

"Do you work in the city?"

"Occasionally." After a lengthy pause. I wasn't sure that I wanted to talk with him.

"Only occasionally. You're lucky. Wish to God I could do my business from home and only occasionally make this trip into the city, but the thing about public relations is that you've got to be where the action is, and all the action is at Madison Avenue. Know it?" His voice pleasantly modulated, a confident voice.

"I've shopped in it, or passed through it. But I don't know it." Keeping my voice noncommittal. Wishing he'd be discouraged enough to return to his newspaper or sleep.

"Keep it that way, my friend. It's a jungle." Yet immediately lamenting himself into a conducted tour of the mysteries, difficulties and near genius of soft-selling an idea, masterminding it into a believable reality. Combination writer, seer and magician, to hear him tell it. "My friend." He'd said it again. Maybe it was only a manner of speech, habitual as a facial tic and just as meaningless. Particularly as I did not feel the least bit friendly. Not there and then. Not to him.

"What about you?"

"I beg your pardon?"

"What work do you do?" Persistent as hell. Me making the decision, to talk or not to talk with him. Deciding, then, selecting the discussable.

"I'm a writer." That was enough for him, the public activity. Giving nothing. He was free to sign off.

"Oh, great. What kind? Journalism?" Giving it lots of enthusiasm as if he'd suddenly encountered a kindred spirit.

"No. Books."

"Great. Great. Books. Anything published?"

"Yes."

"That's great. Great. Should I know any of them?" Hitching up his neat slacks to pluck an invisible speck of fluff from his knee. The train jerked to a sudden stop. Seated with both legs forward I was able to brace myself quickly and safely, but my neighbor was thrown roughly against the seat in front of us.

"Shit!" The expletive escaped him as he tried to save himself, the spectacles knocked askew to dangle from his left ear. He righted himself, removing the spectacles to examine them carefully, turning to me with, "Sorry about that. See what I mean about this train?" A handkerchief in service for polishing the lenses. Blowing on them. Polishing again. His eyes now revealed as pale blue, slightly protuberant. The fingers holding the spectacles smoothly pink, nails neatly trimmed and polished. An inch of striped shirt sleeve displaying golden cuff links, everything in harmony with the suit. The tie fashionably wide, of dark green woolly material. Neat. Perhaps all part of the Madison Avenue image. The hair, the clothes, the expletive.

"Not American, are you?" My neighbor had returned to the subject of me. Legs straight this time for safety, but crossed at the ankles, his elegant brogues a glossy dark brown.

"No."

"Thought not. Something about you. Your accent. Your manner, perhaps. Something." Giving the words just the right lift to make a question out of it. But not quite. Waiting for me to add the rest. Me not helping. Quiet. Watching him and noticing the struggle to follow through on the friendly overture. Expecting him to give it up.

"British, I'd guess," he went on. "Yes, British. The inflection you place on certain words." A hesitant smile exposing itself but ready for instant retreat. Yet even in that moment investing his face with an appealing ingenuousness.

No answer from me. I was playing it cool, as I'd promised myself, consciously fixing my face into a withdrawn, superior aspect, then immediately realizing that I was doing no more than imitating him. Them. Their usual contemptuous, superior attitude.

"It is British, isn't it?" He wouldn't leave it alone. Okay, here goes.

"Inevitably, I suppose. Most of my life was spent in Britain." A bloody speech, by God.

"Oh, so you're not British by birth." Making it both question and statement.

"No."

"Okay. Let me make a guess. The West Indies." Friendly. Smiling.

"Guyana."

"Guyana. Guyana. Yes. That's West Africa, isn't it?"

"No, South America."

"Right. Now I remember. Yes. Dr. Jagan. That's his country, isn't it?"

"His and three-quarters of a million others."

"Right. Right. I once read a piece on him in a book by Arthur Schlesinger on the Kennedys in the White House. Quite an interesting piece. Then sometime afterwards I saw him on television. Not Schlesinger. Jagan. Very handsome and articulate, and so plausible I was half persuaded to his point of view. The Marxist bit put me off, though. But, boy, was he loaded with charisma! Indian, isn't he?"

"Dr. Jagan is Guyanese."

"But wouldn't he consider himself Indian?"

I was becoming a little bored with it, with his insistence on demonstrating how well he knew all about it.

"We are all merely Guyanese."

He gave me a long, questioning look, as if debating the advisability of further conversation. He looked away from me, his fingers interlocked but restless. I thought he'd finally signed off. Roger and out. Muscles in his jaw tightened a few times as if he chewed on some tiny residual fragment of breakfast. I wondered about his own origin. Whatever it was he was evidently secure in it. Once again the train jerked us forward, but this time we were prepared. Through the forward doorway a blue-uniformed conductor widewalked his way along the aisle, checking tickets and placing the punched stubs under the plastic band conveniently located behind the headrest of each seat. His short, bulky body casually adjusted to the bump and sway, while habit made his clippers an unerring extension of the large, spatulate-fingered muscular hand. He checked our tickets and moved on.

"Did you study writing in England?" My neighbor's voice and manner as pleasant as ever.

"No. I never studied writing." That was enough. It would certainly spoil his well-ordered Madison Avenue day if I told him about my first book, a best seller no less, translated into more than a score of languages. Hell, let him go right ahead being condescending.

"What I mean is, was English your major at college?" He was still with it.

"No. I read physics."

"Physics!" Surprise saturating the pause. "Why do you say you *read* it?"

Christ! There I'd done it again. Why did I bother to mention it, then have to be bothered explaining?

"In English universities one speaks of reading a subject." Making it as simple as possible for him.

"Oh. You studied in England?"

"Yes."

"Where?"

"Cambridge."

"Cambridge? The university?" Giving the words the same burden of astonishment he'd used with "New Canaan." His mouth opened in preparation for another question or comment but closed on it. Slipping off his spectacles he favored me with a naked look, as if weighing me to the final ounce, evaluating me for the implied intelligence. The thing inside me was alive, throbbing.

"Cambridge. The university." Letting my voice convey exactly what I thought. The sudden reddening of his neck told me he'd got the message. I could feel his abrupt retreat. So this was the end of the pseudo humilities, the careful circling of each other. He shifted his position, looking outward towards the aisle as if to put as much distance as possible between us. Perhaps he'd have liked to leave, find another seat, but was held captive by the full compartment of a speeding train. Captive. The thought amused me. He'd just have to bear it. I leaned against the corner and studied as much of his profile as his new posture allowed.

"What was *your* major?" Asking the question as soon as I thought of it. Directing my voice to his half-averted face as if unmindful or unaware of his retreat.

"Me? Oh, I did a liberal arts degree." Turning slightly towards me with the answer. "Georgetown University. Then two years at law school."

"I always wondered about the qualifications necessary for public relations," I said, giving it a smile to color it friendly.

"I, ah, wouldn't call liberal arts a particular qualification for public relations, though I suppose it gives one a broad enough general base. As a matter of fact it was during my service stint that I got the idea of going into public relations." Readjusting his position inward once again. I said nothing. He wanted to talk. "I was in the Air Force. Desk job in Rome. Working on what amounted to promotional material. Developed a flair for it, you might say." Returning my smile with interest, the flush disappearing as quickly as it had appeared. "Served with my unit in Naples, Paris, Berlin. Traveled all over Europe. Must say that in those days being an officer had its advantages."

"I know."

"You were in it, the war?"

"Yes. The Royal Air Force." I could not see his eyes behind the glasses but the wordless open mouth told it all.

"The British Air Force?" Again. Just like "New Canaan."

"The Royal Air Force."

"As what? I mean, doing what?"

"Aircrew."

"Flying? I never heard there were any blacks in the British Air Force."

"The Royal Air Force." Really patient with him. "There were quite a number of us. From Asia, West Africa, Guyana, the West Indies. Quite a number." Casual as hell with it.

"In black squadrons?"

"No. No black squadrons in the Royal Air Force. Just crew members. Pilots. Navigators. Bomb aimers. Flight engineers. Wireless ops. Gunners. Ground crew. The lot. Officers. Erks. Everything."

"Officers?" Finding it hard to digest.

"Yes, some of us were officers."

"Funny thing, but I'd never thought of the British Air Force as integrated."

Come to think of it, neither had I. Because at that time the word "integrated" had no special social or political significance. One joined and served. Same billets. Same training. Same uniforms. Same risks. Same enemy.

The conductor hurried through the compartment announcing the next stop. Pointlessly, I thought, because all the passengers seemed comfortably settled for the whole journey to New York. The train slowed, then stopped. I tried peering through the window, but the accumulated grime on the panes defeated me. I leaned back, thinking again about my neighbor's question. Was the R.A.F. integrated?

Memory selecting and etching into sharp focus that first day at the Aircrew Receiving Centre, students and youthful nonstudents milling around in the macadam courtyard of the once-stately residence in St. John's Wood. All nervous as hell but vainly hiding it behind the little we knew. Students arrogantly silent except for an occasional quip deliberately directed over the heads of the nonstudents. They, in turn, loudly airing their Air Training Corps knowledge of airplane silhouettes, map reading, Morse signaling and life. Accents crisscrossing. Welsh. Irish. Scots. Midland. Northern. Cockney. A small group seated in a corner over a noisy card game.

"Raise you half a crown."

"Your half-crown and up a half a crown."

"Cheeky bugger. I think you're bluffing."

"Try me. That's five bob to see."

The sudden shrill sergeant's voice marshaling us into casual order, then sending us off alphabetically to take our medicals. The agony of standing naked in line in a dim, drafty corridor. Clothing in a neat bundle held protectively in front; none of us comfortable in this exposure. Anything to mask our disquiet. The loudmouth claiming he knew all about it. His brother had done it a year ago and told him everything.

"They check you for everything, see. They even have this gadget for looking down your earhole. And the M.O. puts this rubber thing on his finger and sticks it up your bum and reams it around to see if you have anything wrong up there. V.D. or anything. Then they give you shots. Two. My brother said they have these two huge syringes full of stuff. Two for each bloke. They jab them into you, one in each backside."

"What for?"

"Oh, just in case you've got something which they don't spot right away. My brother said some blokes can't stand but one. With the second they keel over. Out cold."

The ribald jokes whispered to and fro.

" . . . so this Jewish bloke goes in to the M.O., unbuttons his fly and lays it on the M.O.'s table.

'Please, sir, will you look at this?' he says, and the M.O. looks at it and tells him it looks okay and what's the problem and the bloke insists that the M.O. examine it thoroughly. So the M.O. puts on some rubber gloves and really gives it the old once-over and then he says to the bloke, 'I don't see anything wrong with it. What's the problem?' And the bloke laughs and says, 'Oh, no problem. Isn't it a beaut?'"

A snigger or two then a voice from farther down the line, "Last time I heard that the bloke was a blackie." Self-conscious laughter near by. Me not caring.

Too much had happened to me too quickly. On first coming to England the word "blackie" had easily set me off. It had suggested the Englishman's contempt for my color. I'd never heard it in my native country. Black. Colored. White. Indian. Those were the familiar words. Perhaps the order was White . . . Colored . . . Black . . . Indian. Funny about that. The White was always first. Top man on the totem pole with everyone else looking up his arse. Some of the blacks wanting so desperately to be white. Setting so much store by what they called their "fair" complexion. The pale skin moving them, they thought, nearer to the white. Thinking of it now, the white men must have had themselves a wonderful time, choosing the black women they wanted, laying on them the staff of acceptance. The fair-skinned blacks or coloreds becoming heir, in time, to the better job, the status, the position, preferred to their darker peers.

Then the other side of it. The black scholars going off to the English universities and returning, inevitably, with their English brides, contributing their bit to the colored thing. Was it leveling up or down? Then the stories filtering into my consciousness. The colored students hopping off to England and being suddenly shocked into the realization that, in the eyes of the British, they were black, English fathers, mothers or grandparents notwithstanding.

Coming back, not cured of their illusions, but considerably chastened. Caught flat-footed in the fallow middle ground during the rise and thrust of political unrest, the blacks emerging as the real power factor, literate, aggressive and determined. Joining with the "other blacks," the Indians, to forge an effective front against the colonial power.

Even though it was then a colony, British Guiana, we the people were proud. Numerously black. Proudly black. In spite of the privileges he enjoyed, the white man was no more than a man. Governing us. Yes. In control. Yes. But we did not fear him. When dreaming my ambitious dreams I never saw him or thought of him as an obstacle or barrier to their fulfillment. In all the days and years of growing up from childhood, nobody, not a single one, had ever told me that the white man would prevent or interfere with what I wanted to do, or be. To be sure, I'd never ask any of them to help me. All I wanted was to be left alone to make my own way. Hell, if I needed anything or anyone, there were the members of my family and my friends. Black like me.

At University in England the situation was dramatically reversed. I was alone. Missing family and friends but determined to drown that loneliness in study. Determined to succeed. Seeing the whites, the English, in a new light. White porters at the college. White waiters in the dining halls. White waitresses in the coffeehouses. Garbage collectors. Policemen. Roadsweepers. Ditchdiggers. Chauffeurs. Shop assistants. Barmen. Servants. In far off British Guiana they were served. In their offices. In their homes. Everywhere. I'd grown up seeing them served. Demanding service. The blacks serving.

In England they did not loom large as masters. Merely people. Rich or poor. High or low. Just people. I had no particular feelings about them. Perhaps the time of my arrival in England was of some significance. War with Germany had just been declared. All around were the hasty preparations for defense, national and personal. B.B.C. news bulletins were high-priority listening as one eagerly and fearfully followed the German rake's progress. War was in the air, the basic topic of conversation. "England expects."

Not me. I was a student and I studied. Came the news of German troop movements and the new word "blitzkrieg." Everywhere the sight of sandbagged buildings and the mounds of earth as families dug themselves protective shelters.

Everywhere the sight of workmen digging. For communal shelters. Individual families hastily throwing up little earthworks around sunken Anderson shelters. Everyone burrowing for safety. News of massive evacuation of children and the aged from the major cities to the comparative safety of the suburbs and countryside. The call for fire wardens and air-raid wardens. Notices of rationing. Coupons for food. Coupons for clothing. Gradually feeling the unease, the threat from over there. Collecting my gas mask and with it the fear of death approaching unseen, unheard.

News of the first bombs. The unfamiliar, fearful sounds of air raids. Reports of raids on London. Birmingham. Southampton. Far enough away from Cambridge. Up to London one Saturday. The chaos at Liverpool Street Station. People frantic to escape the city. Caught in the excitement and fear. Suddenly hearing the air-raid sirens, my stomach curdling at the penetrating sound. Caught in a blinding rush, following others. Whistles blowing, arms pointing. Hurrying down half-darkened stairs into a damp basement room. No idea where I was. No sound of whatever was happening above ground. Everyone talking. No names. Calling each other "mate." Myself included. Much later led out into the sunlight and the swirling dust of near-by wrecked buildings. Police and firemen everywhere. Other men with armbands directing us, urging us along, away from the bomb damage.

Someone beside me inviting me to come along for a "cuppa." Following to a coffeehouse in Aldgate, the rough language hard to understand but warming, comforting. My dark blue blazer with the college crest attracting some little attention. Someone saying, "Guess you'll soon be in it, eh, mate?" between sips of the hot, brown char. Making it seem quite natural that I was a part of the whole, similarly threatened, similarly vulnerable, similarly needed.

Back at college thinking about it. Hearing the talk of fellows who'd "joined up." Three from the rugby team, including the full-back, so what's to be done about replacements. Then two of the younger lecturers. Into the air force. News on the radio of dogfights over London between German aircraft and our own Hurricane pilots. Our own. I was using the term. Even thinking it. Others talking of the University Air Squadron. Joining. Not a word about it in the letters to my mother. Certain that by the time I knew anything about flying the war would be over. Finally writing to tell her. Making it seem like something everyone had to do, without exception.

Now hearing all this bull around me made hardly a dent on my consciousness. The thought of two huge, liquid-heavy syringes blotting out everything else as the line slowly shortened towards the inevitable lighted doorway. The fellow immediately ahead of me already a lighter shade of pale. Funny, I could see that he was scared. His tight jaws and the bloodless area around his mouth, making his lips seem made-up. Gray-red. I had the edge. None of them could guess anything about me. No eye-rolling, shivering bullshit. Just quietly calm inside my black skin. They couldn't know that the thought of the huge syringes waiting inside had already filled my bladder near to bursting. Somebody said they took a urine sample. Sample! I could give them a week's supply.

Inside there was no sign of a syringe. Not yet. Two medical orderlies doing the preparatory work. Checking our height and weight. Looking at our feet. Through a doorway into another room. The M.O. small with bifocals. Fat like Billy Bunter. His gloves cold on the skin. Blood pressure. Eyes. Ears. Genitals. Have you ever had V.D.? No. Any skin disease? No. Then the rubber-finger bit up the bum. Painful as hell. Fear tightening the sphincter. The bugger seemed to like to feel around up there. Into an anteroom with two huge, metal wash basins, grasping the tiny vial for the urine sample. Filling it but impossible to stop the flow. Opening both taps and giving the amber flow company down the drain. Cold water from both taps. Into another room for inoculation. That bloody liar outside. Small syringes. Bend over and an orderly threw the needles into you like he was practicing for a dartboard contest. One in each backside. Hardly hurt at all. Dressing hurriedly, fingers now quite numb from the heatless rooms. Back to the corridor, all faces bravely smiling. Nothing to it.

Marching everywhere, the sergeant's voice a persistent metronome. "Lef' Right. Lef' Right. You, over there, pick 'em up." Marched to a long wooden shack for a meal. Single file to receive the slopped helpings. Meat really long dead. Potatoes mashed into a grayish glue. Everything creamed over with an indescribable gravy. Revolting, yet it all went down. That and the rubbery brown pudding. I was too hungry to taste it. Too hungry to care.

Finally marched off to be formally inducted into the air force. Issued uniforms and the special white cotton flash to be worn on the front of the forage cap, a sign to all and sundry that we were the chosen, the successors to those dauntless ones who had written their own fleeting epitaphs thousands of feet above the lowly earth.

This was it. Months ago I'd joined the University Air Squadron. To learn to fly. That was all. Now here I was, an aircrew cadet in the Royal Air Force, and the progression seemed completely natural.

Sent to a subsidiary airport in Sussex to await posting to aircrew training. Marching everywhere. Waked each morning long before the autumn sun dared raise its head into view. Physical Training on an open drill ground, the cold penetrating deeper than the M.O.'s finger. Teamed up with cockney Jerry Loader and Irishman Bobby Grice. Lectures and films on V.D. The unspoken threat hanging over our heads. Pick up a leak and you're out of aircrew. News of the tragedy at St. John's Wood. A cadet had been associating with two local girls. After posting to his training unit he'd discovered he'd caught gonorrhea. End of the road for his flying ambitions. The following night he'd visited them and killed them both. Butchered them with a knife.

Daily classes. Theory of flight. The combustion engine. Meteorology. Maths. Triangle of velocities. Elementary radio transmission and reception. Morse code. Simple stuff. When do we get on to flying, we all wondered. Rifle drill. Rifle range. Pistol range. Map reading. Cross-country running. Football. Rugby. Cricket. Athletics. Church parades. Everything done impatiently. The test on the flight simulator. Holding the joy stick lightly, following the signals in the earphone. Every day filled with movement.

Finally the examinations. Then the results. And the postings to the training units. Cranwell for me. Luckier ones overseas. Canada. The U.S.A. Everyone excited at the thought of the wings. Everyone sure of making it. Hell, if you flunked the P.N.B. (Pilot-Navigator-Bomb Aimer) you'd still be in aircrew. Say our good-byes. The last night drinking too much beer, singing the bawdy songs at the top of our voices. Full of the idea of courage. The real thing would come later. Jerry knew all the words.

Tight as a drum
Never been done
Queen of all the fairies.
Oh, what a pity she's only one titty
to feed the baby on.

Poor little fucker he's only one sucker
to gnash his teeth upon.

Cranwell an institution. Established. The training tough. Six in the morning to five in the afternoon. Classes. Drill. Firing range. Games. Unarmed combat. The hard, sectional bed a welcome relief each night. But after the study periods. Theory and more theory. More flight simulators. Feeling strong and fit. On top of everything. Going up. Up. The early boyhood ambitions had not included this, but here I was. Sure, my studies at Cambridge were interrupted. But I'd survive this war. Of that I was sure. Then I'd go back and get that doctorate. Nothing could stop that. It just had to happen. Meanwhile the life was great. Lots of friends. Doing things together. Competing. Ability, intelligence, aptitude the only criteria. Different from the others in color, but not thinking of it. Never feeling handicapped by it. That very color giving me the edge with the girls. Unfair exotic odds, Jerry Loader called it.

Everything great, except for the Church parades. How I hated them. They always reminded me of my childhood and that mental image which, even now, is conjured into being by the mere word "church." Myself a small boy, standing beside my mother in the little church in Camp Road, Georgetown, British Guiana. Listening to the hymns sung so enthusiastically by the congregation. The full-throated baritone of the white minister soaring high above the rest. The Reverend Gordon Smith. All clear and detailed in my mind's eye like a sharply etched television playback. Me struggling to keep singing pace with the grownups, but losing them as my juvenile fancy rode with the words and their literal meaning:

Whiter than the snow,
Whiter than the snow,
Wash me in the blood of the Lamb
And I shall be whiter than the snow.

Looking up at my mother's hands, the smooth tapered fingers spread to support her hymnbook. Rich satiny brown. Looking down at my own. Imagining them covered deep in blood. Sheep's blood. Shuddering at the remembered sight of two lambs butchered for the wedding feast of a neighbor's daughter. The frightening thought of being covered in blood. Washed in blood. My ears, my eyes, my mouth, my hair. The rank-smelling stickiness all over me. Then turning white. Not pinky white like the Reverend Gordon Smith. Milky white. Spotty white. Sick white. Like the lepers I'd seen often in the street, their faces, arms and legs ravaged white by the disease. Horrible. Rampant imagination churning my stomach to sickness. Pulling insistently at my mother's dress to be taken outside quickly before everything overflowed. Later, home in bed, warmed by her love and a bowl of tasty broth, trying to explain about the hymn but not making much sense of it. Much of the sharp terror had been flushed out with the sickness. Soothed by her patient attempts to explain the allegory. Obediently accompanying her to church thereafter until, at fourteen or fifteen, I was old enough to say I didn't like going to church. She was loving enough to let me stay at home with my books.

Church parades and weekend passes. The lucky cadets had relatives or friends within reasonable range. What the hell could I do with a weekend pass? I'd tried it. Stayed in London at a Forces Club near Russell Square. The food no better and the helpings less generous than at the unit. Not much fun wandering about during the day and less in the blackout at night. Alone. Another time tried it with Lofty Pine and Ken Yarborough. Dancing at the Astoria and Lyceum. Then seeing the girls home. Underground to Hampstead and only a quick kiss for all the trouble. Missing the last train and the irritation of that long walk back. Better off back at the camp playing penny poker or sitting in the cinema. Wisecracks sharing the action with the images on the screen. Advising the hero on how to deal with the heroine. "Get your finger in, mate." Funny as hell, the off-screen dialogue.

One wet Sunday going by the station bus into Lincoln with Frenchy Pearl and Johnny Conklin. A cathedral town, but dead on a Sunday afternoon. No cinema. Not even a coffee shop. The few people about wearing their off-to-church look. Our metal-tipped boots striking sparks from the cobblestones. The stranger approaching. Gray face, gray suit, gray eyes. Speaking.

"You young men looking for somewhere to go? Would you like to attend a séance?"

"A what?" From Johnny.

"You sit around and talk with spirits." From Frenchy.

"Sure. Why not? Where's it?" Eager.

"Come with me, then," said the stranger. We followed him down the road a few hundred yards to a tobacconist's shop. Next to the shop a narrow staircase led upstairs to an apartment. He knocked on the door and it was opened by an elderly woman as gray as himself. He whispered to her and called us in. About four other people were in the room, one a heavily built, pleasant-looking girl. About eighteen, I guessed. Everybody exchanged names then we all had a cup of tea while we, the newcomers, were briefed on procedure. After the tea things were cleared away we took our places around a large table, each one holding a hand of his neighbor palm down on the table. Frenchy and I sat on either side of the girl. Press gently on the table and concentrate, the gray man had said. I caught Frenchy's eye. Yes, I was pressing gently on the table, on the girl's left hand, slyly massaging the palm with my fingers, feeling the soft dampness. Now and again there would be a convulsive shudder as she tried to pull her hand away. I wondered if Frenchy was doing the same thing. A quick look showed she was red in the face. Everybody else concentrating, eyes half-closed. Johnny sandwiched between two huge blonde women, his hands lost beneath theirs. One of them breathing audibly, the perspiration in bright droplets on her forehead and face. Concentration.

The girl was quietly pulling to extricate her hand. I leaned near and whispered, "Don't. You'll break the circle."

"Quiet," from the gray man.

Without warning the girl exploded in laughter, snatching her hands away to cover her face. All the eyes popped open.

"Get out," the gray man said. Meaning the three of us.

"You coming, too?" Frenchy asked the girl.

"Leave her alone." The gray man shouted. We left. Lincoln on a Sunday afternoon.

Life was good. The studies. The games. The flying. Especially the flying. At long last up there. Dual controls, but feeling the plane respond to stick and rudder bars. Stomach displaced as the instructor made climbs and tight turns, but holding it in. Learning. Living for the day until it arrived. First solo flight. Taking her up, up. Alone. Free. Like a king. Hardly heeding the tinny voice of ground control in the earphones. Bringing her in for the first time. Alone. A little bumpy but thumbs up from the instructor. Flying. Flying. Map reading. Flying. A little farther afield each time. Working to

25

the flight plan. Ground speed. Wind direction and velocity. Air speed. E.T.A. Living flying. Eating flying. Eyes fixed on a distant blue horizon.

Graduation. Passing-out parade. Wings and the posting to Operational Flying Training. Flying and more flying. More speed. A little aerobatics thrown in. Alive. Invincible. Finally the posting to a squadron. Leaving the old friends. Making the acquaintance of a new and constant companion. Fear. That little gremlin who rode unseen in the narrow cockpit. Who ever said that fighter planes were built for one?

Was the R.A.F. integrated? For me, in those days of training and operational flying, the question did not arise. I was at one with everything. A part of everything. Black and different as blonde was different from red. The color of my skin was no weight on my shoulders. I was proud in my skin, not defensive of it. There was a war on and I was a warrior. War drew the people together. Rich and poor. Educated and ignorant. High and low. Color? It seemed to give an extra dimension to me. White rankers saluted. White civilians were very friendly. Here and there the nasty quip about blackies, especially when I was escort to an attractive woman. I ignored those quips, savoring the jealousy implied. They must wish they were me. With the woman. Or wearing the wings. Especially the wings.

One night in 1942, hundreds of us, service personnel and civilians herded together in the Underground at Piccadilly while German bombers raided overhead. Air-raid wardens directing, pleading, cajoling the crowds into some semblance of order along the narrow concrete platforms beside the shiny steel rails, temporarily de-electrified, yet menacing. Lying or sitting wherever space allowed. Faces barely discernible in the dim light. Impromptu sing-songs and bawdy jokes failing to mask the worry and fear or the faint repetitive shocks as bomb after bomb exploded far overhead. The thick concrete wall cold against our backs. Huddled so close together, conversation was inevitable. The one on my left a civilian. A woman.

"Hello."

"Hello." Another, a man, leaning forward around her to declare his presence.

"Jim. My husband." The woman said. "James Proudy. I'm Betty."

"Glad to meet you. Mr. Proudy, Mrs. Proudy. My name's Braithwaite."

No handshakes. No need, pressed together as we were. An air-raid warden balancing himself on the very edge of the platform, begging everyone to move farther along to make room for others.

"Stationed near by?" asked Betty.

"Not very far. Hornchurch. Came up to see a film. Just got here when the sirens started."

"We were on our way home on the bus when the sirens went. The air-raid wardens stopped the bus and made us come down here. This could go on for hours, don't you think?" The anxiety thick in her soft voice. About thirty or thereabouts, at a rough guess, the Midlands accent very pleasurable. Hair could be any color in that poor light. Not much clearly noticeable about any of us. Service uniforms or drab civilian clothes. Pale faces.

"Been in long?" from Betty. "The R.A.F., I mean."

"Eighteen months. Feels like forever."

"Volunteered for that lot, I did," Jim said, leaning forward, his face angled towards me, "but they turned me down, 'cause of me ticker. Well, guess we can't all be ruddy heroes, eh, mate?"

"Don't know about the heroes bit," I replied.

"I keep telling him everybody can't be in uniform," Betty said.

"Anyway, what he's doing is just as important to the war effort." Pride in her voice.

"What's that, Mr. Proudy?"

"Sorry, mate. Mustn't talk about it. Never know who's listening, do we?" Laughing with it.

"Anyway, I always say thank God for you boys," Betty added glancing at me.

You boys. The blue uniform and the wings and the men who wore them. Together. Inclusive. Integrated? Perhaps not in the limited terms of today's meaning of the word. Black and white. More. Much more. At the airport there was the general camaraderie, the particular friendships, the occasional dislikes and irritations of men with men, but all peripheral to the special squadron unity, each appreciating his dependence on the others, his need of the others. Brotherhood. Away from the station civilians saw the uniform and the wings and respected the men who wore them, seizing each opportunity to express that respect directly. Perhaps subliminally they felt the brotherhood. The black ones merely a part of the whole, even if they added an exotic touch to the uniform and the wings. Made to feel welcome, into pubs, into clubs, into houses and into hearts. Invited to participate, to share even the minimal allowances of food which underlined the civilian contribution to the promised blood, sweat and tears.

Christmas Eve, 1942, and those of the squadron within easy reach of home and family already dispersed for two or three days of welcome respite. Subject to immediate recall. For the rest of us the prospect of ample Christmas fare and the improbable pleasure of our own unavoidable company. Later that day I saw the hastily typed sheet on the notice board, bearing names and addresses of local residents offering an open invitation to any airman remaining on the station to share their Christmas lunch.

I picked their name at random, perhaps because I liked the simple sound of it; perhaps because their address was within easy-walking reach of the airport. If things became dreary I could easily excuse myself and return to the station. After all, one could always amuse oneself there with dancing, the station cinema or the ubiquitous poker "school."

On the way there I wondered about them. Why were they doing this? Perhaps no children, so this was one way of doing the extra bit. Perhaps a son or sons in the services far away from home. Prisoners of war. Or dead. There had to be a reason. How would they react to seeing me? Well, Christmas was always full of surprises, so I might well be theirs.

Just to keep things balanced I bought some stuff in the N.A.A.F.I. canteen, things which were in very short supply for civilians because of rationing. A pound of ham, nuts, tea, chocolate. Made a Christmas package complete with seasonal wrapping paper.

The house was an attractive cottage in a quiet side street in Brentwood. Privet hedge still darkly green adding a touch of privacy. Rosebeds centered in a small lawn in front of the house, the thorn darkly threatening even with nothing to protect. They were both at the door to welcome me before I could touch the doorbell. Must have noticed my approach. He tall, gray-haired and stockily strong. She not much shorter, buxom and brown-haired. Smiling their welcome and their protest over the parcel.

This was new for me. Different from going to the flat of a popsy one met at station "hop" or picked up at the cinema, the Masonic dance hall or a local pub. This was formal, or nearly so. No, Mrs. Rowlands. Yes, Mr. Rowlands. Even leaving out the name didn't help much. They struggled awhile with Flying Officer Braithwaite, until Mrs. Rowlands protested and asked, "What's your first name?"

"My friends call me Rick."

"May we?"

"Of course."

"All right, Rick. Now you must call us Elsie and Dan."

I tried but couldn't do it. Those gray hairs, I suppose. So I did my best to avoid using any name. Over lunch we talked, but it wasn't easy. I did most of the talking, responding to their questions about the country of my birth, the people, the climate, the politics, the products. Everything. Then about me. My parents. My boyhood. My schooldays. My reasons for coming to England. My studies. On and on. So busy fielding the questions that most of the food remained untouched. Mrs. Rowlands noticed this and read it the wrong way.

"Sorry about the meal. I had no idea what kind of things you eat."

That killed what little appetite remained. I'd wait just long enough to allow for courteous retreat then get the hell out of there. Perhaps they imagined I feasted on raw missionaries or something.

"Anything else I can get you? Some eggs? Ham? Anything?"

I assured her that I was fine and I never ate much anyway. No dessert. Coffee was okay.

After lunch we sat before a roaring coal fire in their living room and talked some more. Me with my eye on my watch. More questions.

"You speak excellent English, Rick," Mr. Rowlands said. "Where did you learn it? What's the native language of British Guiana?"

"English," I answered, somewhat shortly, furious with myself for having misjudged the notice on the board. These people had really invited a white airman. They'd expected someone like themselves. All this rubbish about special food and native language as if they supposed I'd just fallen out of the trees. The irritation was growing in me, pulling me away from them.

Perhaps Mrs. Rowlands sensed my mood. She suddenly switched the talk to themselves. They wished their own sons were alive today to help in the defense of England, but the twins had been stillborn two years after marriage. No other children. Mr. Rowlands was an engineering draftsman now on special assignment with one of the ministries. Too old for active service. Three nights each week both of them served as local air-raid wardens. Without a break in the recital she said, "Dan, why don't you take Rick to the basement and show him your models?" Then to me, "They're really lovely."

I made sounds about the time and needing to catch a bus back to the airport, but she insisted there would be others and he led me off. The entire floor space of the basement was arranged as a workshop, the wall nearly covered with racks of shiny tools. Close together in the center of the floor were a power lathe and workbench. Elevated to the height of the workbench and following the perimeter of the room were twin tracks for a miniature railway system, complete with signal boxes and switch gear, all controlled electrically from a panel on the workbench. The models which all worked were scale replicas of past and contemporary steam engines. They were lined up neatly on the workbench.

He had made them all. Everything except the wheels which he bought from a dealer in model parts. They were more than toys. With them he tested various theories he had on compression ratios and interactive levers, occasionally making alterations to the combustion system to achieve better results. Absolutely fascinating. We played around with the trains until Mrs. Rowlands called us up to tea. I'd forgotten about leaving. He invited me to come over any time to help him with his experiments. Said the advice of a physicist was just what he needed.

Over tea some more talk but this time about general topics. Churchill. Rationing. The best time of year for planting in the kitchen garden. When I got up to leave they extracted from me a promise to visit them again. Soon. Next Sunday.

Back at the station I thought about it and was not sure that I wanted to see them again. Well, not just see them, but spend all that time with them. Difference in age or something. And all those questions which made me acutely aware of the difference between them and me. Black and White. On the camp I was just me. At least nobody asked me any crappy questions. I ate what everyone else ate or I'd go hungry. Christ, over lunch when Mrs. Rowlands asked, "Do you feel the cold much? I mean, does it bother you?" I felt like answering, "About as much as it bothers you." But I couldn't be rude to her in her own home. Hell, I wasn't complaining about anything. Snow or sun. Why couldn't they just accept that I'd feel like them, eat like them, behave like them?

Several times during that week I thought of phoning them with an excuse and each time postponed it, arguing with myself that they were charming people and I was perhaps making too much of questions simply asked without ill intent. Then Sunday arrived. Too late for excuses. So I was there again. Me and another N.A.A.F.I. parcel. This time it was better. Easier. After lunch we went walking through the woods on the edge of town, the leaf-laden ground soft from recent rain and frost. Overhead there was the occasional rumble of aircraft. Their home was in direct line with the flare path of the main runway. Yes, this time it was better and they were great company. We talked about books, the theatre, about what would happen after the war. I told of my intention to return to University to complete my studies. The things I would do afterwards. Experimental research. The time passed. Quickly. Again the promise to visit them. This time flying duties prevented me. For three weeks. The end of the second week Mrs. Rowlands telephoned. Saturday evening. The first telephone call I'd had since joining the squadron. They wanted to know if I was all right and when would they see me. I explained that my duties were temporarily changed and I would be in touch with them as soon as it was convenient. The middle of the next week I received a letter from them. Just a short note saying they hoped all was well with me and remembered me in their prayers. Come and visit us soon.

So it was. Bit by bit we were drawn together. At least once each week I'd spend an afternoon or evening with them. Sometimes helping Mrs. Rowlands in the garden, but mostly with her husband and his experiments. Eventually they asked me to let them stand in for my mother and dead father. Just for the duration, they said. It wasn't easy, even though by that time I was aware of their kindly interest and responded to it. How could I call a white woman "Mother"? Once again she solved the problem. I noticed that they began addressing each other as Mum and Dad, instead of Elsie and Dan. Without thinking about it I was soon doing the same thing. They suggested that I bring some of my friends over, and occasionally there'd be several of us sprawled on the living-room floor or in the basement with Dad. Fellows and Waafs. Mum would make them welcome but would leave no doubt that I was special. For my part, it was wonderful to know that there were those two who cared about me, even worried about me. I was no longer alone in England. I grew to love them dearly and their own love comforted and supported me and survived the most exorbitant demands which, in time, I unwillingly and helplessly made upon it.

Integrated? The word had no relevance to that time and those circumstances. In the face of the very real threat of a German invasion hands were linked in a common effort and the color of the hands was unimportant. As I had been a student happily pursuing my studies without concern about my color, so I became an airman. Period.

The train drew away from the station.

"How long were you in?" my neighbor asked.

"Pardon?" Pulled back to the present, beside him.

"The air force. How long did you serve?"

"Five years."

"Then you began writing?"

"No. I returned to University."

"I'd thought of doing just that," he said, "but before my separation from the Air Force I made a few contacts back in the States and got an offer of a job. I often wonder what life would have been like if I'd gone back to law school. How did it go for you? Were you able to adjust easily?"

"I managed." Leaving it there. Courtesy did not require that I unravel my life for his inspection.

Adjusting had not been easy, but it was rough for all of us. All those who had skipped part of their youth for the cruder activities of killing and being killed. Now we were back. Divested of the uniform and the medals and the wings, we were ordinary, inglorious and even a little out of place among the new crop of undergraduates. Older. Wiser, perhaps. Impatient with their posturings. Intolerant, and a bit jealous of their flaunted youth. To them, we had so quickly become obsolete. Already they were moving towards a new age of aircraft design and jet propulsion.

It was extremely difficult to switch from the fear and excitement of living in the shadow of death to the prosaic but far more demanding world of lectures and books and study assignments. Especially in those first days and weeks after demobilization when the euphoria from routine and control gradually gave way to an acute feeling of dislocation and loss. So very often I thought of chucking it and trying for a job with my bachelor's degree, but Mum and Dad would provide a patient, restraining influence. They'd remind me of my mother's faith and her high hopes for me. Their own persistent enthusiasm was a gentle but forceful prod against my own doubts and indecisions, Dad arguing and persuading, assuring me of my ability. Telling me I had a special talent and it would be criminal waste to neglect it. Sounding so much like my schoolmaster, way back in the early boyhood days of British Guiana.

Eight years old and struggling with the mystery of elementary science. Richard R. Persico. So readily his name springs to mind. Tall, slim, narrow-faced and ascetic, the thin, flexible wild cane in his hand like a drill sergeant's baton. Carefully he'd explain a geometric theorem or algebraic equation, and thenceforth the swishing cane would provide an agonizing spur to concentration and understanding. The palms of my hands were often red-streaked and inflamed reminders not to make the same errors twice. At home my mother would tenderly apply a cooling salve while quietly assuring me that it was all for my own good. "One day you'll look back on all this and be grateful to Mr. Persico." How often did I hear that and the other familiar bit about abilities which his perceptive eye had discovered in me and he was determined would not go to waste. Him at school. My mother at home and myself in the middle, loved and painfully encouraged. Exulting with each academic success, forgetting the hurt each time my teacher pridefully said, "I knew you could do it." England and University glowed dimly in the far distance, but attainable. Living through the other years, home and mother far away in another continent, in another environment, bridged by the letters with their burden of love and encouragement. Always that special tidbit of news: "Mr. Persico asked to be remembered to you," and "I read in the newspapers that Mr. Persico is leaving teaching for the priesthood," and "Mr. Persico left yesterday for Africa." Later my own letter to him at Achimoto College in Ghana and his reply:

> ... my concern is not with the possibility of your success in the examinations which lie before you. They will offer you no more than a challenge to display your ability. My hope is that you remember the Biblical parable of the talents, and bear in mind that that situation could easily have been reversed. The servant with the five talents might have become careless in the abundance of his gifts and so, wasteful of them ... my prayer is that He will bless you with a full sense of responsibility for the gifts He has so lavishly bestowed upon you ...

Even from that distance his words were as sharp as the old stinging cane. The times I read that part, "They will offer you no more than a challenge to display your ability," as I waited nervously, fearfully for the published results of the tripos, telling myself I'd done enough, and yet not quite sure until there it was. I'd passed. But the war was on. 1940. The R.A.F. pilots in their Hurricanes were writing other challenges high in the blue over Cambridge. Lecture rooms and books suddenly were for the faint of heart. Youthful ambitions were shelved. For five years life was measured in moments. Today was everything. Tomorrow was half-hidden behind Messerschmitt 109s and Focke-Wulfs and antiaircraft barrages and vapor trails and stalled engines or locked undercarriages or blanketing fog. Until 1945 and once again there was today and tomorrow and ambition and plans. Now. Sitting again in the lecture rooms, but restlessly, thinking of those who didn't make it. Marveling at my own good fortune. Struggling to make the books and the lectures mean what they used to mean. Hearing in my mind the haunting words of that far away ascetic, " . . . responsibility for the gifts He has so lavishly bestowed upon you . . . " Feeling already old in a situation designed for youth. Finally putting it all together and once again my name on the published lists. Again the dream of achievement as a physicist. Once again riding high on hope because things were happening right for me. Confident in the examinations. Without worry. Well, not too much. Then there it was. Celebrating with Mum and Dad. The congratulatory cablegram from my mother. Mum giggly from the extra gin and tonic. Dad prescient about success ahead. I was fortune's child, marked for truly big things. And me believing it all. Making plans on the half-realized dream of achievement as a physicist. Dreaming. Then the bitterness of seeing the dream whittled away, bit by bit, day by day, into weeks and months, until the only place on the whole arid horizon was a mangy schoolhouse beside a bomb-racked, rotting graveyard, and a smelly classroom with forty-six foul-mouthed youngsters. White, English youngsters.

"When did you begin writing?" this one beside me asked.

"1958."

"1958? What were you doing in the meantime after leaving college?"

"Nothing and teaching."

"Teaching? In England?"

"Yes."

"Physics?"

"No. English literature."

"But you qualified as a physicist, didn't you?"

"Of course. Degrees and all that. Even planned a doctoral program."

"Then why didn't you pursue it?"

"Oh, I pursued it all right. As far as I was able to. Let me put it this way. I was made to realize that there were no openings for black physicists."

"But you were British, weren't you?"

I was getting bored with these bullshitty questions. Where the hell had he been living all his life? Hadn't he heard or read anything about his English cousins? Or the German or Greek or Italian or any of his other white immigrant antecedents? Was he suddenly blind? Christ! Why the hell was I even bothering to talk to him?

"One of the lessons I finally learned from my years of living in England," said patient me, "was that I was British but not a Briton. I hope you see what I mean."

He made some adjustment to his position, leaning towards me and crossing his legs with care. Everything in order. Even his voice, as he said, "Are you absolutely sure that your color was the dominant factor in your failure to find a position as physicist? Isn't it perhaps, well, possible that your qualifications, however good they were, might not have been exactly what were required?"

Perhaps that was the way he prepared his public relations stuff. Picking the words and placing them side by side. Like matching shells from the seashore. Dead things. Perhaps he thought he was impressing the hell out of me.

"It's possible."

"Then how can you say . . . ?"

"Because they told me that was the reason. Generally it was hinted in terms sufficiently clear to leave me no doubt. On one occasion they even spelled it out for me . . . "

Seeing it in my mind as clearly as if it had happened only yesterday. That first job interview. This one beside me easily could have doubled for one of them, the four-man interview board, all pink, smoothly well-groomed and courteous, my degree transcripts and the letter from the Higher Appointments Office spread on the table before one of them, the chairman. Chatting very affably with me about my country, my early education, the R.A.F., my work at University, my interest in research. Making me comfortable and hopeful with their show of friendly interest. Then coolly, casually knocking it all over with, "Mr. Braithwaite, I'm sure my colleagues would wish me to say that we are deeply impressed with your qualifications and your obvious abilities. Were the circumstances different we would be only too happy to appoint you a member of our staff. But we have a problem. All our employees are British and we would face the reality of their almost certain reluctance to work with and perhaps under a person of color. To give you the appointment would be to risk disruption of the balance of good relationships which has always been a particular boast of this firm . . . "

More and more of the same, all of it adding up to "No." Remembering other things about that interview. Not one of them had seen me before I entered that room. Nothing in the information spread before them had given the least hint of my color. Even my name sounded quite British. Yet the chairman could so confidently express their collective opinion and decision. One look at my black face and they'd known their decision. No consultation necessary.

I'd gone into that room with my spirits high and my confidence intact. On the crest of my belief in myself and my abilities. Certain that I'd be hired. Everything had encouraged me into thinking so. The people at the Higher Appointments Office who had talked with me and introduced the firms to which I had applied. The quality of the work I had already done. My place on the examination lists. Among the first five. God! What more did they want? I thought I'd done it all. Everything that was required to prove myself. In the laboratory. In the examination. Those talks I'd had with my professors. Their praise of my work. What did it all mean? Did they know even then that the doors would be firmly closed against me? Were they even then saying to themselves, "Go to it, black boy. Do your stuff. Enjoy these moments while you can, for this is as far as you go." No. I couldn't believe that. I mustn't let everything be colored by one bloody experience.

That was at the beginning. Shock. Surprise. Anger. I felt all those, yet my determination rode high. If that was the way they felt, to hell with them. There must be other firms, other potential employers who would be more interested in what I had done as an indication of what I could do. I'd find them.

My applications went out and the invitations to interviews came in. I followed up each one, stubbornly refusing to believe a dark skin would be so important to so many people. Surely they couldn't have all got together and agreed to keep out black scientists. At home I reviewed each interview and my responses to the questions I had been asked. I researched the questions at the library to cover any area I might have missed. I anticipated other questions and prepared myself to deal with them. I argued with myself that perhaps it was not my color which bothered them. Maybe it was my accent, unfamiliar and perhaps unwelcome to their ears.

But nothing changed. Interviews and rejections. That was the pattern. That and the other thing. My confidence in myself. Gradually but inevitably the fear of facing those interviewers. Not fear of their carefully incisive questions. Not that. But the terrifying fear of freezing up under their sweetly patronizing scrutiny, or perhaps of exploding under it. Finally abandoning that level of search for the openings advertised in the newspapers and trade journals. Abandoning the interview boards in plushly furnished offices and boardrooms, for the personnel officers in metal-furnitured utilitarian surroundings.

Discovering the same rejection, even though it now came from a considerably weaker vantage point. Now I was resented for what I knew, the way I dressed and spoke. I was an oddity. A black man with a master's degree and cultured speech who'd flown Spitfires during the war. Applying for work at their level. On several occasions the interview hardly touched on my technical qualifications.

This one beside me on the train was so much like those personnel people, so sure of himself. Behind his steel-rimmed glasses a near twin to that one at Ford's, Dagenham. I'd sent my application and received an invitation to appear for interview. Woke early that morning and prepared myself, mentally reviewing every possible question likely to arise. Not forgetting the snide digs I'd come to expect, but telling myself to keep cool. Don't show anxiety because those bastards loved to have you anxious. The little fish like to chew on littler fish, as the saying goes. Cool, but dignified. Dressing with care. Suit carefully pressed. Shoes polished. Everything in order.

I was there a few minutes before the stipulated time and went through a barrier at the main gate. Two uniformed gatekeepers in their little office.

"Looking for someone?" from one of them. The stupidity of it. As if I'd be there to admire the view.

"I'm here for an interview." Very crisp.

"With Personnel?"

"Yes."

"What name?"

"Braithwaite."

He consulted a typed list on a clipboard then said, "Yes. Mr. Covington. For ten o'clock. You're early."

I said nothing. It was ten to ten. He pushed past me to stand outside the door. Pointing towards the mass of buildings, he said, "Stay on this path. It's that building straight ahead. You'll see the sign on it. PERSONNEL. You can't miss it."

I followed his instructions, en route aware of the hiss and pound of the huge automotive works in the distance. Inside the Personnel Office a blonde young woman sat behind a large desk with intercom equipment and a single rose erect in a narrow-necked glass vase. She showed some surprise at my entrance.

"Yes?" Her gray eyes made a slow comprehensive survey of me. All of me.

"Mr. Covington, please." He was the man who'd signed the letter to me.

"Is he expecting you?" She asked. The upward lift of her thick eyebrows reinforcing the negative tone of voice. It occurred to me that if the gatekeeper had a list of expected interviewees, so should she. Perhaps she was merely going through the motions. Acting her role in the pecking order.

"He is." I replied. Resentment beginning in my insides.

"What name did you say?"

I hadn't said. Deliberately I paused a moment before replying.

"Braithwaite. E. R. Braithwaite."

Painted fingers of her left hand flicked switches on the intercom while the other hand held the telephone handset tight against her face. After a short interval she said, "Mr. Covington, there's a Mr. Braithwaite who says you're expecting him." Every word conveying her own doubts and suspicions to the unseen listener, meanwhile keeping her eyes on me. Soon she replaced the handset on its cradle and stood up, saying, "Will you come with me, please?" the unexpected courtesy sounding like an epithet. I followed her down a corridor to a door with the name "L. P. Covington" and inside. Waving her hand towards a chair, she continued through the room to another door, knocked and entered. After about a minute she re-entered the room and walked out of it without as much as a glance in my direction.

I was not alone in the room. There were three others. All men. All very professional looking in dark business suits, white shirts and regimental ties. All ex-army. Youthful, but with the hard look of experience beyond years. Each of them gave me a quick stare, but said nothing. Perhaps I should have worn my air-force tie. Evidently we were in an anteroom waiting to see the same person. Mr. Covington. I wondered whether we were all there for the same reason, competing for the same job, or were there several jobs each requiring different qualifications? If there were only one job, what chance did I have against them? To encourage myself I looked each one over. Told myself there was nothing there to be concerned about. Each one looked as palely nervous as I felt. Could be, each one needed the job as desperately as I did.

With a white skin they were free to choose, so if they were here it must mean that they were not qualified to try for the better jobs. So with my qualifications I should have the edge. The advertisement was for a research assistant, with at least a B.Sc. degree. I was offering more. Much more. B.Sc. Honors and a master's degree. I wondered how they saw me. What they were thinking about me. Could they guess about my education, my qualifications? Or had they with that quick, cursory glance dismissed me?

The little gremlin who always appeared at such times perched himself on the edge of my mind and advised me to get up. Leave. Why waste time? Hadn't this thing happened enough before? Why go through it again? But my need for the job overruled him. This might be the day and the place. I'd never know if I ran away.

The inner door opened. From behind it a voice called a name and one of the young men got up, entered the room and closed the door carefully behind him. The others looked at each other and at me. I wondered whether the neat NO SMOKING notice on one wall was deliberately intended to increase our nervous state. Most servicemen smoked, and these two must be itching for a cigarette. I was lucky. That was one habit I'd avoided so far.

About fifteen minutes passed and the inner door opened again to let him out. He closed the door, picked up his coat and left, nothing in his face or manner offering any clue to what happened to him. A few minutes later the door opened and another name was called. Another of the waiting men disappeared inside.

"Times like this five minutes feels like a lifetime," the remaining army type said. I looked at him, surprised out of my reverie, but could think of no fitting rejoinder. He said no more. In about ten minutes he was called into the room as the one who had preceded him there left. In what seemed no more than five minutes he reappeared, looking tense. Not even glancing at me he went away.

Every sensory area in my body was poised for the call. Five minutes. Ten. Fifteen. Half an hour. The door remained closed and I became acutely conscious of the ticking of my watch. The gremlin was laughing loudly deep in my ear. After forty minutes had passed the door opened and the voice called, "Braithwaite."

That should have told me what to expect. Up to now it had been "Mr. Greville. Mr. McLaine. Mr. Bowden." My nervousness disappeared, in its place the sudden, throbbing anger. Perhaps he'd opened the door then hurried back behind his desk. By the time I entered the room he was seated, my transcripts and curriculum vitae spread before him.

"Won't you sit down?" he said, inclining his head towards the chair placed in front of his desk. I sat. Through steel-rimmed spectacles he looked me over very carefully then returned his attention to the papers on his desk.

"Fighter Command, I see," he said, lifting his eyes to peer at me, tapping the papers with a yellow, rubber-ended pencil. I nodded. No need to answer. It was all there for him to read. The slim fingers of his left hand teased the curling ends of his blond moustache. I noticed his tie. R.A.F. I wondered in which branch of the service he'd been active. Not aircrew. Not with those glasses.

"Five years," he said. No word from me. I'd learned from experience to say as little as possible, even to direct questions.

"Not so easy for some of you Brylcreem lot now in civvy street, is it?" His eyes were on me. I noticed that their focus was slightly off center, somewhere over towards my left shoulder. The little gremlin's laughter was shrill in my ear. I set my teeth together, holding tight against the thing in my chest trying to spill itself out. I'd come here to talk about a job. Not the Royal Air Force.

"What has any of that got to do with the job you advertised?" It was all I could get out, the rage crowding me.

"You sure you want a job here?" he asked, leaning back. Toying with me. At his ease.

"I'm sure." If there was the least hope of getting the job I didn't want to blow it.

"You don't look to me as if you needed a job." His eyes running over me. My suit, shirt, tie. Whatever he could see from where he sat.

So here it was. All hope suddenly gone. The gremlin quiet. I said nothing, quietly despising him. Perhaps he was waiting for me to say "please." His attention once more on my curriculum vitae, then again raised to me, mocking me. Tapping his teeth with the rubbered end of the pencil.

"Anyone who could afford to dress like . . . "

I didn't wait for the end of it. Rising carefully from the chair to stand near his desk, high over him. Leaning across to collect the papers and the large manila envelope which had contained them. Seeing the way he paled and quickly leaned away from me. Seeing the sudden fear in his eyes. Having no intention of touching him. Replacing the papers in the envelope and walking out of there. Doing it without a word. Anxious to be away from there quickly, lest the murderous rage overtake me and I tear him apart.

Afterwards walking aimlessly about, not seeing, not hearing, not feeling. Later that night arriving home but not talking about it to Mum and Dad.

At their invitation I'd gone to live with them after coming down from Cambridge. During the first months everything was fine. Just like those wartime afternoons and weekends. Helping Mum in the garden. Working in the basement with Dad on his models. Discussing my plans for the future. I'd written to my mother about my intention to find a job in physics research and continue with my doctoral studies. Dad and Mum were delighted. We'd dawdle over dinner talking about my ambitious plans. In spite of the five-year interruption of my studies through war service, everything was working out beautifully. I was on top. Confident. Enthusiastic. Wartime developments in electronics had opened the communications field and research was the thing. My field. At long last the studying and working would pay off.

Mum and Dad encouraged me. Sometimes at night we'd take a stroll through Loftis Lane to the local pub, the King's Head. Have a pint or two with a gin and tonic for Mum, chat with some of the locals, perhaps join in a game of darts, then back home. Easy. Comfortable with them.

Now it was all changed. We weren't talking any more. Well, not in the old way. After each interview, with each rejection, they became somewhat identified with the others. I was rejected because I was black. My intellect, my abilities didn't matter a damn. All whites saw was my blackness, and because of it they rejected everything else about me. So why not those two at home? Sometimes, after an interview the very thought of returning to them was an ordeal. The irony of it! Going home to whites to tell them of the crushing cruelty and contempt of other whites.

I continued to live with them because I told myself I had nowhere else to go. Nowhere else I could afford, that is. I was still able to pay them the little they would accept for my board and lodging, so I could persuade myself I still had my self-respect. I had my meals with them as usual but gradually things were changing. Further and further I retracted into myself. Mealtimes became painful. For me, and no less so for them. I'd hurriedly down the food, hardly tasting it, then hide myself in my room. Always with the excuse of studying, though the long hours were spent on my bed, awake, reviewing every moment of the latest humiliating experience.

They never suggested that I leave. Never said or did anything to make me feel unwelcome. On the contrary, they made all kinds of overtures in their attempts to restore the former happy situation. Mum devised tempting dishes, within the limits imposed by rationing. She mended my shirts, darned my socks, cared for me. Dad enticed me with pleas for help with his models. He had an ambitious plan for converting them to electricity, and claimed that he needed my advice on the circuit designs. I'd go down with him but my heart was not in it. The bitter irony was that while silently rejecting their overtures I felt responsive to their efforts to reach me. Responsive but resistant.

Things got gradually worse. I hated sending the useless applications. Hated the invitations to interviews when they came. Hated the rejections which followed. Hated the whites who rejected me. Looking back, it seems certain that everything and everyone that came anywhere near me must have been tainted by my bitterness and hatred. I must have carried it around with me like some poisonous miasma, careless of and insensitive to whatever effect it might have had on others. No one mentioned it. Not even Mum and Dad. No one.

Not till that day after I'd been through another fruitless hour-long charade of an interview. That morning as I was about to leave home Mum had stopped me at the door and said, "I don't think you should go out today." I reminded her that I had an interview in the city. She replied, "Would it make any difference if you didn't go?" As if she knew what was happening to me. But I insisted on going, even though I knew she was right. I didn't want to let myself accept that she could so fully understand my pain.

After the interview I walked, aimlessly, but needing temporarily to lose myself in external sights and sounds lest I hear the clamoring of the hate inside me. Aimlessly through the Strand and Piccadilly, walking, into Green Park, and tired. I sat on a bench, wallowing in my misery, plumbing its very depths to discover me, perhaps, at the bottom. Asking myself why, why I kept on attending those interviews. Idly watching the half-wild ducks cavorting on the pond, letting the minutes slip away because I was in no hurry to go home. Not even looking up when a man sat down near by. Hearing the rustle of the paper bag, the clucking sounds he made to attract the ducks, the gentle jolt of the bench with the throw of his arm. His chatter a continuous stream until I looked up to discover whether there was someone else near him or if he was really talking to the ducks. No other person in sight. Catching his eye but looking away. He was white. I didn't want to know him, to hear or see him. But too tired, too dejected to move away.

He got up and went to squat at the edge of the pond for closer chatter with the ducks, feeding tidbits to a few. Then back to the bench, but this time near to me. Talking. Not addressing any remark to me, just talking. Me not listening. He could have dropped dead for all I cared. Talking, as if he were hungry for an opportunity to say something to someone. Anyone. Talking, till I couldn't help hearing some of it. About how people could be hurt by other people and things, but most of all by themselves. Stripping themselves, tearing themselves until their spirits were laid bare like an exposed wound, unprotected and unprotectable. On and on. All sorts of philosophical rubbish. Then he said something to me, I can't remember what it was, but it got under my skin.

I turned to him angrily and said, "Look, why don't you shut up? You white people are all the same. All this philosophical drivel has no meaning because, in fact, you are white and when you look out on the world you see it in a certain way. For black people like me it has to be different . . . " And without realizing it, a lot that had been building up inside of me began to spill over onto him and I began telling him about going for interviews and being rejected because of my black skin. He shut up and listened. I wasn't really concerned that he listened, but once I began to speak I couldn't stop myself. After a while he turned to me and said, "You know, I'm not surprised you didn't get any of those jobs. You walk around in hate. It's all over you."

And then he began to talk to me and gradually I found myself listening. He asked, "Why don't you try something else? A man like you, with your educational background, shouldn't think that physics is the end of the world. Try something else." Often he would say, "a man like you." And he began to tell me about the London County Council and their need for teachers. "A man like you would be welcome." I said, "I'm not a teacher, I've never been trained as a teacher."

"Oh, don't worry," he said. "With your university background they'd reach to get you."

I listened. I didn't want to be grateful to him. I even hated myself for listening to him; but what he was saying was making sense in spite of myself. He talked and talked and I decided inside myself that I would give it a try. But I didn't tell him so. I couldn't even afford to say "thank you" to him. I let him talk and talk and afterwards I got up and walked away. But I phoned the London Council the next day and I got the job.

"Did you teach college level?" My neighbor asked.

"No. Secondary school."

"Would that be about equal to our high school?"

"More or less." I'd never thought about it.

"Any problem about your color?" he asked.

"My color is always a problem. For some people." I wondered if he was trying slyly to needle me.

"I mean, was there any resistance to you, from faculty or from students?"

"There's always resistance. Some members of the faculty were friendly and helpful. Others not. The students were something else."

"How did you get on with them?"

"We had a rough beginning. Rough."

Remembering my very first morning at that school. I'd arrived early to present myself to the headmaster as his new staff member sent from the Divisional Office. From the street I had to cross a macadam forecourt to reach the main entrance to the school. This forecourt served as the school playground. Bunched together near the center, a group of girls was tossing a netball to each other and noisily protesting at the efforts of two boys to intercept it. They gave no attention to me as I walked around them. In attempting to grab the ball one of the boys collided heavily with a girl who promptly let loose a flood of swearing, each word succinctly, degradingly clear.

They were all members of the same social class to which I found myself assigned.

"In what way?"

"They were, all of them, antiauthority. Antipolice, antiparents, antischool, antiteachers. I was black, an unfamiliar extension of the authority they disliked."

"Were you the only black teacher in the school?"

"At that time I was the only black teacher in all of London. Yes. I was quite a phenomenon."

"Why didn't you quit and try another school?"

"Because I couldn't afford to quit. It was the first job I'd found after nearly sixteen months of searching. It wasn't the kind of job I really wanted, but at least it relieved me from exposure to the tiresome round of rejections. Anyway, I'd no intention of quitting under pressure from a bunch of children. Hell! I'd once ordered men. In any case, staying there became a challenge. A personal thing."

"Couldn't you use some form of punishment to restrain them?"

"Not in that school. Punishment of any kind was taboo. The headmaster believed that teaching should need no 'fear supports.' He believed that if a teacher was sufficiently skillful and imaginative he would discover ways of making his efforts effective without resorting to punishment."

"And you accepted that?"

"I really didn't care one way or another. I wanted the job and, at the time, I would have agreed to support any kind of philosophy to get it. I believed myself strong enough to cope with anything, no matter what it might be. I was not interested in philosophies or concepts. I would have tried teaching a cageful of apes if the possibility were offered."

Saying that and remembering that that was exactly how I saw them, at first. Uncouth, near-illiterate and casually cruel without that animal's inclination to lofty dignity. Seeing them thus and hating myself for being so easily victimized by whatever fate threw me into that situation as their teacher. I was not trained as a teacher. I was a qualified physicist denied the opportunity to practice my skills in a country for which I had voluntarily risked my life. Before eventually getting the job as teacher I came close, awfully close, to being completely demoralized. The casually contemptuous way in which my applications were dismissed at one level because of my color, and the equally contemptuous proposition that I was too well qualified for work at a lower level, eventually soured me to the point of hatred. Bitter hatred. Of those who had so contemptuously used me, and, in time, of all who looked like them. All whites.

"Why didn't you try somewhere else? Return to Guyana or come here, to the United States?"

"Guyana? In those days it was still a British colony. White Britons still occupied the positions of influence and power. I would have been jumping from the frying pan into the fire. Or so I thought. The United States? The published stories of the treatment American blacks received did not commend your country to me. Anyway, I suppose I lived with the hope that someone would eventually say, "Mr. Braithwaite, we're sure we can use you." Isn't it odd? I consider myself an intelligent man. I'd got the teaching job, but to me it was merely a temporary thing. A stopgap, you might say. I went right on hoping for an opening in communications."

"And hating?"

"Yes. And hating. It was not something I wished upon myself."

"All whites?"

I looked at him, wondering what the hell he was getting at. Why was he so preoccupied with my hating? That was all a long time ago. A long bitter time ago. Since then I'd been trying to live above hate instead of merely living with it. Talking with this man, this stranger, about those times and circumstances brought the memories flooding back and memory, in turn, stirred the old sensations. Oh, yes, hating some whites was only the beginning. Incipiently, before I realized what was happening, it had grown and spread itself to influence everything I did, to touch everyone I knew.

"Yes," I told him. "All whites." Why should I be apologetic to him?

"I find that hard to believe," he replied. "Someone like you. Educated. Sophisticated. There must have been some exceptions. At least someone." A sly smile playing around the corner of his mouth. Perhaps all this was part of his public relations technique. What the hell did he know about it? I was no less educated and sophisticated when others like him had rejected my application. And since when did he know I was educated and sophisticated? Since the absence of other seats had forced him here beside me. The bullshitting hypocrite. Suddenly into my mind popped the face of that old man in the park. The thin mouth forming the words as he told me a few truths about myself. Realizing now that I'd not hated *him*. Irritated at first, by his ceaseless chatter. Then, dare I think it, grateful to him. Funny. I'd not realized that until now.

"How long did you teach?" my neighbor asked.

"I was a teacher for nine years."

"Nine years! Well, I guess you found it wasn't too bad. And so you abandoned physics after all?"

I looked at him, wondering at the cool effrontery of the man. He'd taken the seat beside me reluctantly, then he'd started the conversation. Now he was pursuing this questioning as if he had every right to probe wherever he chose. He'd approached me as carefully and watchfully as a predator in unfamiliar territory. Now he was relaxed, smiling with his questions. How could I allow myself to forget that he was still the predator? How deep was the smile? I debated with myself the advisability of bothering with him. Of leaning back and closing my eyes and to hell with him. Treat him as if he weren't there. Let him taste a little of the contemptuous rejection they were so proficient at handing out. Why not? But then, wouldn't that be following their familiar lead? I'd always prided myself on courteous conduct. Why make an exception here merely because of his stupidity about sitting beside me? If courtesy dictated answers, it did not dictate their content. So I'd be courteous. But his type of questioning strained courtesy to its limits, particularly his way of plaiting a question into a statement.

"I've never abandoned physics. I merely used my scientific training to achieve other ends." Smiling at how neatly I was packaging the response, but knowing that the truth was much more than that.

Physics had abandoned me. The doors to a career in that field were closed. Tight. In my heart I knew it, even though a perversely errant seedling of hope insisted that I continue sending applications far afield to the northern industrial centers. Receiving the invitations to interviews with the tempting money orders for the return fare. Then playing my own private game. The short letter acknowledging receipt of theirs and offering to appear for the interview on a date conveniently distant. Ten days to two weeks. Enclosing a recent snapshot of myself so they'd match the black face with the credentials and make up their minds. Saved myself a lot of traveling. The snapshot did it. No replies. I'd head homeward at the end of each teaching day hoping to find a reply and knowing there would be none, yet bitterly disappointed at my own accurate appraisal. Finally accepting the obvious. Writing no more applications. No more study sessions at the library. Bitterness and hate a twin-headed, familiar incubus.

Teaching helped. The routine of waking each morning with the knowledge of having something to do. The sheer relief of it after the long months of waiting and wondering. Untrained in the skills and techniques of teaching I borrowed every available book on the subject. I was paid to teach. I tried learning from textbooks by well-known authorities, but discarded them. They may have been good in themselves, but useless for the special circumstances in which I found myself. So I had to learn by doing. By applying my scientific training to what had become a challenge. Making as complete as possible a record of each day's schoolroom activities, then analyzing it carefully each night, separating the positive elements from the rest. Anything which held their interest even briefly was positive. Any hint of interest from them was positive. Any comment, any question, any observation was positive. I examined it all, looking for leads, exploiting everything, using everything. Discovering their interests and gradually relating these to the requirements of the curriculum. Learning from it, then testing what I'd learned. Variations on themes. No. I didn't really abandon physics. I made it serve my new needs. Not the science of physics, but the discipline of thinking, of exploring, of reaching for the unknown through the familiar. Smiling now at the memory of it.

The London County Council had accepted me on the strength of my academic qualification. They assumed, perhaps with justification from similar appointments, that I knew enough, together with my military experience, to function effectively as a teacher. I shared that view until the first moment of contact with the school and the students. I had imagined them in a classroom setting similar to my own childhood experience—clean, quiet, well-mannered youngsters seated at neat rows of desks, obedient and industrious. In fact I was confronted by a group of rough, untidy, aggressive young adults who made it very clear that they had little use for or interest in academic pursuits. The school provided them with a safe alternative to the streets and harassment from truant officers and the local police, and they intended to enjoy that safety, without interference from myself or any other teacher, until they reached school-leaving age and could "hustle" for themselves.

They greeted my early efforts with sarcastic disdain. When, during the first week, I found occasion to comment unfavorably on the generally poor level of attainment in such basic skills as reading, writing and comprehension, one of them reacted with, "Can I ask you something?"

"Certainly," I replied.

"Okay, then. They put this school here, right?" He turned to his companions, whose support was immediate and loud.

"Right," they chorused.

"And they put all these desks and chairs and books and things here. The blackboards and notebooks and everything. Right?"

"Right." They assented in unison.

"And they pay all you teachers to come here every day. Right?"

"Right." No word from me. No word expected from me.

"And they make us kids come, because if we don't they haul our mums and dads up before the law. Right?"

"Right."

"Okay, then. So the school's here, and you're here, and we're here. But who says we got to learn anything, eh? Who says?"

"Right. Who says?"

I was neither impressed nor bothered by that, because at that time I did not grasp the simple yet profound truths hidden in his argument. It was my job to teach, and I assumed that if I taught, they would learn. But first I had to learn how to teach, in spite of the things they said about me. Deliberately intended to be overheard. Blackie. Chimney Sweep. The Black Knight. Tar Baby. Never in direct address to me, so I took no action. But seeing the parallel, even in that crummy locality, with the same things I'd hated in the well-dressed, soft-spoken members of the interviewing boards. Even these underfed, underhoused, undereducated inhabitants of a social slag heap imagined they could sneer contemptuously at my black skin and the human spirit it housed. And yet, in spite of all that, something was happening to me. I was caught on the treadmill of knowing the rightness of my hatred, seeing it supported all around me, inside and outside the school, yet feeling it undermined and eroded by these same youngsters and myself helpless against the erosion. The way I dressed, spoke and conducted myself interested them, because it was quite different from what they had expected of someone like me. They would ask, "Do people in the country you come from all dress like you do? Are all the people in your country toffs? Are they all very wealthy people, because you look like a wealthy person? Do all the people in your country speak as you do?" In the very nature of their questions something was emerging, their respect for what I represented coming through grudgingly. Because I was so different from what they had imagined black people would be. University graduate. Fighter pilot. Officer.

I would tell them about my country and its people, showing

them similarities as well as differences between their lives and ours. And this is where my dilemma really pinpointed itself. The more respect emerged, the more I was forced to respond to it. And it didn't matter what I did or how I would argue with myself in the quiet of my own room, I could not avoid this. And the other thing which happened at the same time. As this relationship with them developed, I felt the need to talk about it and, naturally it was to Mum and Dad I turned, responding gradually to their unfailing interest in my welfare. I would discuss the classroom happenings with them, and gradually, once again we were talking at home. Mum and Dad and me. It was rather circuitous, perhaps, but necessary. Talking about the children to talk to each other, their love reaching out to me through their simple, matter-of-fact appraisal of the incidents I recounted. And often their comments provided not only encouragement but valuable clues to effective action. Like that incident with Tich Jackson. I'd prepared the lesson carefully. Geography. Covering the course of the Amazon River from source to mouth. The territory through which it flowed and the inhabitants of that territory. Their way of life and the changes through which it had evolved. In brief, I tried by careful research to provide a comprehensive simulated voyage. Illustrated with maps and my own impromptu sketches on the blackboard. Focusing on the children of the territory, their schools, their language, their games and pastimes, their work. Drawing parallels with the East End scene. They were quiet. Attentive I thought. Then a raised hand.

"Yes, Jackson." Delighted that the question was further evidence of their interest.

"What kind of toothpaste do you use, Sir?" As usual, any digression received unanimous support.

"Yes. Tell us. What toothpaste do you use?" From another.

"Do blackies have to go to the dentist? Me Mum says all black-ies have good teeth." And another.

"I seen some blackies on the flicks and they all had these big white shining teeth."

"Is it true some blackies eat people? Me dad says that's why they all have strong teeth." Laughter.

"Go on, Tich, don't be daft." Someone chided him.

"Well, 's what me dad said."

On and on, tossing it to and fro among themselves. Myself frus-trated and angry at the ease with which the carefully prepared les-son had been shredded into nothingness. Even after I stopped the interplay it was impossible to recapture their interest, so I fell back on the old wasteful standby of having them copy exercises from their textbooks into their notebooks.

At home that night I mentioned the incident. "So what did you do?" Mum asked.

"Nothing I could do. Once they're launched on that kind of frivolous question game the only thing to do is end it."

"Why?" she persisted.

"Because they're not really interested in answers. They're stupid and try to fit everything to their stupidity."

"That may be, but your business is to teach them, isn't it? I think that what happened today was your own fault. So don't blame them."

"How do you make that out?" Dad asked her. He, too, was puzzled.

"Look, son, don't forget that some of those children have never set foot outside London. You were giving them a lesson in geog-raphy, weren't you? Talking to them about South America and the people there. All right. They know that you are from South Amer-ica, so I suppose while you're talking to them they're looking at you. They're seeing you as South America. You know, when I was a child at school in Bradford I often forgot to listen to what my teacher was saying. I was too busy looking at her clothes and shoes and if she wore any jewelry. I remember one teacher who always wore a lovely cameo brooch at her throat. I could never take my eyes off it, wondering when I would grow up so I could have one like it. Anyway, perhaps it's the same with your children. While you're talking to them they're looking at you, at your shoes, your clothes, your hands, your teeth. Of course, some of them would be listening, too, but even if they're not, they're learning by looking."

"Yes, Mum, but . . . "

"Hear me out. You remember how you used to tell us about your boyhood in your own country, and how you and your little friends would go wandering in the woods and cut twigs from the black-sage bush and chew the ends into a tuft which you used to brush your teeth? And how the fine ash from a wood fire was great for polishing the teeth? Well, why didn't you tell the Jackson boy the same thing? That would have shut them up. And after that you could have gone right along with the rest of your lesson. Dad and I always found those things interesting, so why not try it out on the kids? That's what I'd do. If they wouldn't hold still for the ordinary textbook stuff, give them a bit of the extraordinary." And that sweet, nimbly laugh which made it all seem easy and not at all as if she were giving me the soundest advice. Helping me through those difficult, frustrating days and weeks and months, unreservedly. Teaching me how to teach without claiming to do so and teaching me love by loving me. More than that. Her suggestions often worked. The next time someone in the class tried that kind of question I stayed with it, relating it to the topic in hand.

Perhaps my training as a scientist helped in this respect. Anything at all that seemed to work even momentarily, I seized upon and tried to develop, so that at first they were not really lessons for the youngsters. Each one of them was a trial piece whose effectiveness I could then observe. And at the end of each day I would make notes and each week I would look through the whole block of notes to see what worked or what didn't work, posing myself many questions. Was it the way I gave the lesson? Was it me? Was it the material? I kept these notebooks carefully numbered in sequence. It's amazing how they accumulated over the years. As my relationship with the class developed positively, as my skill at learning from them, teaching them and holding their attention developed, so what I put into these notebooks changed.

Holding their attention was the thing, and the clue to this I learned from one of them. Another one of those lucky accidents to which I became prone. Mum and my guardian angel helping. It was Mum who advised me to watch my students. "They're watching every move you make," she said. "So do the same with them. That way you'll know what interests them and the best way to teach people is through their interests." For someone who always claimed to have had no more than a secondary-school education, Mum was wisdom itself. I followed her advice. I watched them. I listened to them. I talked with them. But mostly I listened, in the hope that any bit of information about the lives they led outside the school would help me to understand their conduct in the classroom. After all, I saw them for only about five and a half hours of any school day—their remaining eighteen and a half hours together with every weekend and holiday were spent partly in sleep, but mostly in enthusiastic participation in the less formal but more demanding classroom of the streets, where the arts and crafts of survival were learned under harsh parameters of proficiency and loyalty, and where success and failure were determined by the severe judgment of their peers.

In the playground I often overheard heated discussions or arguments involving rapid mental calculations on monies won or lost, borrowed or lent, spent or saved, from students who, in the classroom seemed paralyzed by the simplest of arithmetic abstractions; lengthy, graphic accounts of local adventures to a spellbound audience from boys and girls who, in the classroom, found great difficulty with the simplest exercise in oral or written prose. In the classroom they were, or preferred to behave as if they were, underachievers; in the playground they became, with hardly an exception, inventive competitors. It seemed to me that if I could arrange some level of transposition of interest from the playground to the classroom we might achieve the first steps in a mutually beneficial relationship.

With this in mind I introduced the following idea. Well, let's say I first discussed it with Mum, exposing it to the acid test of her special wisdom. With her blessing I laid it on them. Each morning, immediately after registration and before beginning the first assignment, each member of the class would, in alphabetical turn, address the rest of us without interruption, for not less than five and not more than ten minutes, preferably on some aspect of the assignment itself, or, failing that, anything of particular interest to the person speaking. It occurred to me that, in this way, we would each gain some experience in speaking to a group and in listening courteously to a speaker, apart from learning a little more about each other. Because each student knew from his own copy of the class timetable the subject matter of each day's first assignment, there was the possibility of private research or discussion in preparation for each one's turn, or, even more important, observations of relevance or otherwise of that particular assignment to that student's life or interests. As a member of the class I insisted on my right to participate in this activity. In my turn.

At first the students stubbornly resisted the idea, perhaps because of shyness, or a reluctance to be under such formal scrutiny by their peers and myself, or other reasons at which I could only hazard a guess. However, I persisted with it until they reluctantly agreed to try it for a little while, but insisted that I be the first speaker even though my turn should fall late among the Bs. On the morning of my address the first assignment subject was English history covering a period which dealt with the expansion of Britain's colonial empire. Briefly I spoke to them of British Guiana, my native country and a part of that colonial empire and the fact that, like themselves, I was one of the Crown's subjects. Keeping my remarks very brief I managed, however, to show them that a study of history was really a study of people and the way in which deliberately or accidentally their lives were interdependent. They listened, and afterwards, during the lesson period, questioned me further, obviously fascinated by a definitive relationship between a textbook of their own historical record, themselves and me.

After many painful, humorous and sometimes embarrassing moments, the idea took hold, especially as it seemed to offer an opportunity for showing off.

One of the more lively personalities, Tich Jackson, armed himself with a beautifully illustrated copy of the *National Geographic* magazine to give us an hilariously funny address on the peculiar customs of undress favored by the women of an African tribe, when his turn coincided with a geography period on Central Africa. Some of his comments were perilously near the bone as he wondered how some of his classmates, the girls, would fare if they went to such a country and were expected to adopt the local customs. However, we were discovering each other. Through this means I learned something about their homes, parents, relatives and out-of-school activities, their attitudes to their immediate environment and their concerns on approaching adulthood. Many of them soon demonstrated a flair for easy, confident presentation, timing themselves within the minutes allowed.

Potter was a member of my class. Considerably taller and larger than any of the others, he invariably occupied the back-row seat farthest from my table and beside a window which allowed him an unobstructed view of cracked chimney pots, an occasional flight of racing pigeons and an even more occasional flash of blue sky. Like the other boys, he wore blue denims and tee shirt in summer, adding a zippered windcheater in cold weather and kept his hair so close-cropped that the pink scalp extended his broad forehead well beyond the hairline.

My colleagues had briefed me on Potter the first day I joined the school.

"Leave Potter alone," they advised, "unless you wish him to do some simple chore like moving desks and chairs. If it would do any good we're sure he'd be happy to move the school a few yards this way or that, singlehanded. But don't waste your time and his asking him to do anything academic. He's dimmer than a Toc-H lamp. Good-natured and helpful, but dim. If you insist that he work you'll only upset him, and if you upset him you get on the wrong side of the others. They all call him Dopey Potts, but consider that their special prerogative. No one else is allowed such liberties. He's in school waiting out the last months to his fifteenth birthday, then he's off to work on the docks with his father and will earn more in a week than most of us will see in a month."

That's what they told me, many times, but like most of us, I was anxious to please and impress in a new situation, and I did not leave Potter alone. At least not at first.

When asked to read he would dutifully open his book and, red-faced, run the index finger of his right hand across the page, his lips moving soundlessly. The others would exchange knowing glances and smiles, particularly when I'd interrupt the mime to say I could not hear him. It did not help. He remained good-natured, but inaudible. If asked to transcribe notes from the blackboard or textbooks to his own notebooks, he did it in a neat, clear hand, but when the assignment was creative composition he invariably turned in a blank page. The entries in his arithmetic notebooks were a colorful mishmash of simple exercises neatly and correctly done, within a border of multiheaded gnomes, single-engined aircraft and exotic fish. The top of his desk was covered with these intricate doodles. At any caustic comment from me he'd lower his head over his desk, favoring me with an even larger expanse of scalp and remain that way until I turned my attention to someone or something else.

In time, I left Potter alone. In fact it was not difficult even to forget that he was in the classroom, so adept he had become at rendering himself unnoticed. Even at registration each morning he'd not respond to his name other than to look up from his perpetual doodling and smile.

In due course it became Potter's turn to address us. Usually I placed a tiny red mark against the student's name on the morning of his address; that was the best way to keep track of our progress, and they soon became interested enough to know the routine and be prepared.

The preceding afternoon as I passed through the school gates on the way to my homeward-bound bus, Potter fell into step beside me, his bulk easily dwarfing my six-foot frame.

"Hi, Sir." It was the very first time he had ever spoken to me other than in reluctant response to a question or request. My surprise ran a poor second to my curiosity.

"Hello, Potter." He carried his bulk so easily I wondered if he was good at any games; in the playground he usually lounged against a wall on the periphery of a chattering group, slouched down as if to reduce himself to acceptable size.

"Going to the bus stop, Sir?"

"Yes, Potter. The Green Line stop at the top of Commercial Road."

For someone from whom I had been accustomed to hear only "Yes, Sir" or "No, Sir," he suddenly had become quite garrulous. Curiouser and curiouser. For awhile we walked on in silence, me wondering why the signal honor. Then, "About tomorrow, Sir."

"Well, Potter, what about tomorrow?" Still curious.

"Me mum's got to go to hospital tomorrow and I'm to look after the young 'un. Me kid brother, Sir."

This was a familiar, even routine situation. In their families everyone helped; attendance at school was not the top priority.

"Anything serious?"

"No, Sir, not really. But since the new baby she's got to go every so often for a checkup and that."

"Good. Will she be back in time for you to attend the afternoon session?"

"Oh, yes, Sir."

"That's fine then, Potter. Please give her my best wishes when you go home."

"Okay, Sir." He continued walking beside me, forcing me to quicken my stride to match his easy swing. Then, "About tomorrow, Sir."

"Well, what about tomorrow?"

"I mean about my turn, Sir." The penny belatedly dropped.

"What about it?"

"Only that I won't be able to do it, Sir."

"Never mind, Potter. Someone else will stand in for you, and you can take his place the day after tomorrow."

"No need to do that, Sir, me changing places, I mean. You know me, sir, I don't know anything to talk to them about."

We'd reached the bus stop and I joined the end of the queue with the hefty lad beside me continuing his plea.

"You can ask anybody, Sir, the staff, anybody, and they'll tell you, Sir. No sense in me taking a turn, Sir."

I wished the bus would hurry. Those nearest us in the queue were showing too much interest in me and the pleading youth whose voice sounded louder than I had ever heard it.

"Tell you what you'll do, Potter," I said quietly, "just stand before the class for five minutes. Give them your rank and serial number and go back to your seat." The joke misfired. He merely stared at me as if I were the dopey one.

"What, Sir?"

"Nothing. Forget it."

"Okay, Sir. Can we forget about tomorrow, too, Sir?" He wouldn't leave it alone. Some in the queue were grinning, though I felt sure they had no idea what we were talking about. Perhaps it was his size or haircut. Or the worried look on his round face.

I tried another ploy, whispering, "Potter, everyone knows something about something. So talk for five minutes about, well, your baby brother. Anything. When I was your age in British Guiana, I did things. Hobbies. Games. Anything. And if I got bored I'd cut a green bamboo pole, trim it, tie a piece of string to the thin end, a piece of cork and a bent pin to the other end of the string, fasten an earthworm on the pin and go fishing. Everyone does something, Potter."

But he wasn't listening. The face above me opened to let out a roar of laughter, sudden and loud, drawing from those near us quick, empathic smiles. "You're pulling me leg, Sir," he managed between chuckles.

"Why? What's so funny?"

"You didn't catch any fish with that lot, did you?"

"Of course I caught fish."

He shook his head in disbelief, the face still creased in smiles. "I was only thinking, Sir, that p'raps it's different where you come from. If you try that over here you'd be waiting for your first bite." More laughter from him and smiles from our instant audience.

"An earthworm is an earthworm and a fish is a fish, Potter. What's so special about English fish?"

"Well, you see, Sir, I go fishing and I can tell you . . . "

With a squeal of brakes my bus arrived. Remembering what had started the thing I said, "Okay, Potter, tell me tomorrow." Still shaking his head he left me, and I climbed aboard.

The next morning I'd forgotten all about the incident. Registration was proceeding as usual when I called Potter's name. Not only was he there, but for the first time ever he answered with an easily audible "Sir." Surprising myself and everyone else. Me particularly. What about his mother's visit to hospital? Registration completed, we heard from him again.

"Can I come up now, Sir?" It was usual for me to exchange places with whichever student was to address us. Everyone turned to stare at Potter. All this talking was completely out of character, his character, and they reacted with, "What's he on about, Sir?"

"What's up with Potts?"

"What's coming off with Dopey?" Like myself they'd forgotten it was his turn.

Looking over at him I saw that his desk top was piled high with a collection of magazines, on top of which was a battered felt hat hung with what looked like an assortment of multicolored insects. Near by, two or three long, narrow, canvas-covered bundles leaned against the wall. Potter was ready for his turn, whatever it was.

"Whenever you're ready, Potter."

I went down the central aisle while he came up the side with an armload of books and bundles which he placed on the table. He opened the topmost book at the centerfold and pinned it on the board to expose a glossy colored print of a fish, then from one of the bundles drew some sections of thin bamboo which he quickly coupled together into a flexible rod. He faced us.

"I'm going to talk to you about fishing," he said. Ignoring the giggles and using the bamboo rod as a pointer, he began. "This here is a pike." He then proceeded to tell us everything about the pike— its coloring, the kinds of streams in which it could be found, its usual adult size and rate of growth, its mating and feeding habits, in short, everything it was possible to know about a pike.

"This bloke is carnivorous," he told us. "That means he eats other fish, specially littler ones than himself. Take a gander at those teeth. But he's a bit of a scavenger, too. Will eat any dead thing floating about."

I could hardly believe the evidence of my ears. Potter using polysyllabic words like "carnivorous" and "scavenger," and using them correctly. Potter, the Dopey One, the Wordless One. Dim as a Toc-H lamp, they said. Backward, they said. For the first time in my life I heard of the differing social levels of marine life. Surface feeders and bottom feeders and those who manage somewhere in between. Fish which laid eggs and others which produced their young ready hatched and able to fend for themselves.

There were no giggles. In fact there was no sound except those made by Potter as, without any particular regard for syntax, he kept the class spellbound, introducing here and there an amusing anecdote about his friends, the fish.

Someone nudged my arm. It was the headmaster who had entered by the side door, displeasure in the tight way he said, "Any reason why these children have not had their midmorning milk, Mr. Braithwaite? The crate's still outside your door. Surely you know our rule against punishing them in any way . . . "

"Shhhhhhh . . . " from those nearest us, impatient at the intrusion of his voice.

"What's going on?" he asked, surprised into whispering.

"It's Potter, headmaster," I told him.

"Shhhhhhh . . . " A little more urgently this time. Nudging me to make room for him on my seat, the headmaster settled down, perhaps to find out for himself what was taking place, and was soon as captivated as the rest of us. Potter was in full flight.

The lunch bell was a sudden, insistent interruption, startling us all and breaking the spell of Potter's presentation. Quickly I went up front and in spite of the students' protests, thanked Potter for a truly lively and instructive address and extracted a promise from him to continue it at some future time.

At lunch in the staff room the Head could hardly contain himself; a keen weekend angler, he claimed that he'd learned more listening to Potter than from all the books he'd ever read on fishing.

"That boy. Good God! I'd given up on him. You'd have thought that all there was to him was his size. Loafing around the place like a great lump and never a word out of him. Now this. It's frightening, to think that we're letting youngsters like this fool us with their disguise of stupidity or backwardness."

Contrary to what I'd expected he was very upset, blaming himself and us, his staff, for taking the boy's apparent limitations so much for granted that only by accident we'd discovered this about him. And so late.

"We're the fools," he told us. "We're the backward ones for being so completely taken in. The words he used. The way he spoke, as if that huge head of his was just packed tight with valuable stuff he was bursting to tell. That boy's a teacher, I tell you. A natural."

The students' response was no less enthusiastic. From that day they dubbed him "Fish Professor." "Dopey" was gone. Vanished. Soon wearying of the long name they made it "Professor," a tag which stuck to him for his remaining months at school, and I suspect perhaps longer. Most important, however, was the change in Potter himself. After that demonstration he could never retreat into his former lumpy, inarticulate role.

That experience with Potter taught me a valuable lesson about teaching. As of that day I approached each student as an intellect, unique in himself, differing from others in the nature, content and direction of his interests and knowledge. Some demonstrated a ready flair for academic matters; others plodded painfully through the simple mechanical skills; others had already become quite proficient at exploiting a native acumen and an appreciation of the prevailing social conditions. I noted everything so that I could test it all for leads to more effective teaching. Keeping my notes became my major private activity. In time I not only recorded how the lessons went, I included the things they said in the classroom and in the playground complete with their richly colorful expressions. Gradually I included notes on their conduct, and was frequently saddened by things I overheard or saw, indicative of their forced maturity in a social environment which made few allowances for their youth. Mum's patient wisdom was a continuing source of help and encouragement.

There was that instance with Sapiano. Swarthy, stocky and aggressively handsome, his bulging muscles and freshly shaved face were a bit startling on a fifteen-year-old. He was bright and could be very funny on occasion, usually at my expense. One morning he arrived immediately after registration, apologized and with something of a flourish placed a roll of five-pound notes on my table with the casual remark, "Will you look after that for me, Sir?" and was off to his seat. The white bank notes were held together by an elastic band crossed and recrossed upon itself. It was the largest amount of money I had ever held in my hand. I looked towards Sapiano. He was sprawled in his seat watching me, and it occurred to me that he was waiting for me to ask him something about the money. I opened the drawer of my desk, put the notes inside, closed and locked the drawer and put the key in my pocket. All this had been observed by the whole class. Not a word from me. If Sapiano had stolen the money he would not have acted so openly. He was neither nervous nor afraid. Okay, I'd wait it out and see what happened. By then I'd learned the unwisdom of asking them questions on personal matters. Left alone they'd tell what they wanted to tell. Pressed, they'd shut up. Tight. They'd all seen the money. They knew where it was. I'd be in my classroom all day with it. If Sapiano wanted to tell me anything about it, he'd do so in his own good time, without any prompting from me. If not, he'd take his money at the end of the day, and no questions asked.

I was on playground duty during recess. When the bell sounded I opened the drawer, took the money and placed it in the inside breast pocket of my jacket. They all saw me do it and we all trooped out of the classroom. In the playground they stood about in small clusters or played touch football while I wandered in and out among them, exchanged a word here, a comment there. Milligan was sitting on the stoop as usual reading a brightly colored book of comic strips. I stopped to look at it. He smiled up at me with, "That Sapiano's a case, isn't he, Sir?"

"He certainly is."

"Yeah. A real nut case."

"A case." No whys. No wherefores.

"He's lucky."

"You think so?"

"I guess so. All that dough."

Nothing from me.

"Wouldn't surprise me if it was more than a hundred quid."

"You could be right. I wouldn't know."

"At least a hundred."

Nothing from me. Waiting.

"You know where he gets all that dough, Sir?"

"No. Do you?"

"Uh-huh." Looking off into the distance.

I waited. Nothing more from him. I turned to go. His voice stopped me with, "He's got a bird who works up West." His eyes on me, testing for signs of the impact of his words. I merely smiled and kept moving, my face a mask for the jumble of thoughts his remark had created. Sapiano was fifteen. "He's got a bird who works up west." Freely translated that meant, "He's got a girl friend who is a prostitute in the West End." God! The thought of it. My fifteen-year-old pupil and who? What was his bird like? Oh, well. My job was to teach him, not to hold a watching brief over his morals. As

Mum said, "Set them an example in yourself. They'll take it from there in their own sweet time."

At the end of the day I handed the roll of money to Sapiano, again in full view of the class. From him no explanation. No comment.

Weeks later we were all together in a bus on the way to the London County Council's playing fields in Kent. These playing fields, situated in the pleasant, green, Kent countryside, were used in turn by London secondary schools which, like our own, were restricted to a narrow macadam forecourt for playground space. From Cable Street where the school stood, our route passed under the Thames through the Blackwall Tunnel and into Kent. As the bus made the approach run down a side street towards the tunnel, Sapiano suddenly rolled up one of the windows and shouted to someone on the near sidewalk. The person, an attractive, young brunette, returned the wave, her happily smiling face and shapely figure joining in the action. The whole busload erupted, joining noisily in the greeting. She continued to wave until we were nearly out of sight. In the quiet of the tunnel Sapiano looked at me and said, softly, "That's me bird, Sir."

There were other times. Gayer, more exciting, more satisfying times, as those students grew and expanded and developed before my very eyes. We worked together. I learned about them. Seeing them as intellects and as persons with intellect. Respecting the intellect and the person, more often in spite of, than because of, the superficialities of speech, manner or dress. Many of them lived in overcrowded homes where personal privacy was impossible or nearly so, and the only water supply was from a communal central tap located on the ground floor. And yet each was stubbornly, aggressively whole, asking little of anyone and expecting considerably less. They were intimately familiar with privations yet rarely complained. I, who had been embittered by my failure to find desired outlets, was forced to recognize how far more fortunate I was than any of them. Difficulties and disappointments apart, I was equipped with certain special skills. In acquiring those skills I had learned to think and could therefore deploy my skills to advantage. Self-pity was a waste of time. As all my colleagues agreed, any one of my students would survive in his familiar environment. Many of them would make a fairly good living in spite of limited academic achievement.

Each in his or her own way displayed strength, courage, fortitude. Rita Bernstein, thin, blonde and tiny at fourteen, singlehandedly had assisted her mother in the unexpected birth of her baby brother. Two o'clock in the morning, the baby already on the way, the nearest telephone a public telephone booth half a mile down the road, the next-door neighbor a prostitute her mother would not let across her threshold. So Rita carefully followed her mother's instructions. Washed her hands in hot, soapy water and helped the little fellow out before running the half-mile to telephone an ambulance. Telling it at her turn, the class openmouthed during her recital.

So what about me? What was there preventing me from doing considerably better than any of them, or, at least, as well as any of them? I had a job. My first responsibility to myself was to do it well. I was a teacher. So, teach. Watching, listening, talking to them, I learned how to teach them. In time, I learned from them how to teach.

Month by month, year by year, the note taking continued. Perhaps because in those days I had few personal possessions, I kept each numbered copy safe in a corner of a cupboard in my room, readily available as a source of inquiry. The pile grew until the day I left the teaching profession. The way in which my students and I worked together during that first year set the pattern for those who succeeded them. Our emphasis was on understanding the relationship between the school-day activities and the harsh realities of life awaiting them outside. Together we developed skills and an understanding of the interaction of those skills. Reading words was a skill to be mastered, but insufficient in itself. We also read numbers and drawings and blueprints, so that we would not be afraid to read the word or the sign or the hieroglyphic. We talked together, argued together and learned to be patient and courteous with each other. I persuaded the headmaster to let us visit museums and theatres and ballet and make field trips to art shows and the courts among other places, because we believed that we should be participants in living, understanding the functioning of whatever gave the community its purpose and thrust, direction and stability. Sitting in a courtroom as observer instead of prisoner was a new and strange experience for many of them, and the subsequent discussions disclosed a very perceptive appreciation of the strengths and weaknesses of the law and those who enforced it.

"Tell me about your books." Leaning in towards me, bringing me back to the present beside him. "Did you begin writing while you were teaching?"

"No."

"Then what did you do? Quit teaching?"

I didn't quit teaching, as he put it, but I had no intention of explaining anything to him. Questions. Questions. Saying nothing about himself but pouring the questions on. Well, to hell with that. Every question he asked triggered some of the old memories, the old bitter memories. Here he was, perhaps safe and secure in the job he'd selected for himself and would continue to do for the rest of his working years. He was well fed, well dressed and evidently well paid. Successful. That was the word. I, too, had seen myself in similar terms, once upon a time, had studied to be well qualified to do work for which I'd be well paid and therefore well fed and well dressed. Successful. Success had come, it was true. But not in the way I'd planned it. Not through the means towards which I'd prepared myself. And all because of those, like this one beside me, who had arbitrarily erected the barriers against me, had casually closed the doors in my face.

Because of them I'd been diverted into teaching, hating it at first, treating it as a temporary exercise in survival until something better came along. Even after the first year or two in teaching I still hoped, telling myself I could, without much difficulty, catch up with recent research and developments. Only after five years as a teacher did I finally relinquish any hope of returning to physics. Only then did I reconcile myself to the new profession and seriously apply myself to an appreciation of its demands and responsibilities. I was teaching, so I would be a teacher. And a damned good one. I'd make a real career of it.

I was learning how to teach, how to use the tools available to me. The curriculum was a tool, not a grand design. I used that tool to serve my pupils, to stimulate and encourage their imagination, their interests and their abilities. Textbooks were tools. Field trips were tools. All were intended to be used in the thoughtful pursuit of knowledge, and I was as much a participant in that pursuit as I encouraged and prodded them to be. Demonstrably so.

Word got around. Inside and outside the school. Parents visited, supposedly to discover what was responsible for the change in their children. Some of them were evidently suspicious of a "blackie" teacher who was having so much influence with their youngsters. Others put a severe strain on my courtesy by their patronizing airs. Some merely wanted to see the man who was their children's chief reference. "Sir says" had become a familiar refrain, and they wanted to see who "Sir" was. Some expressed surprise to find nothing startling or strange in the classroom or its equipment. Or me.

Teachers from other schools came along to chat with me. They had known of the school's earlier reputation as a hangout and sanctuary for near-delinquent adolescents. They had heard that changes were taking place and they wanted to see and hear about them. Some were very encouraging. Others expressed doubts about the practicality of a situation which allowed pupils to challenge the teacher on academic as well as other issues. That the challenges were made intelligently and courteously weighed very lightly with them. We even had visits from overseas teachers in Britain on sabbatical. The London County Council sent them to observe and question us.

It may have been this publicity which eventually separated me from teaching. After nine years in the profession I was asked by the London County Council to work as advisor in the Council's Child Welfare Department. During the early postwar years considerable numbers of immigrants were attracted to Britain because of widespread reconstruction and the boom in skilled and unskilled employment. These immigrants were whites and blacks from independent as well as colonial countries of the then British Empire. Australia, India, Pakistan, Canada, West and East Africa, the West Indies and Guyana. Apart from these colonials and ex-colonials there were a number of aliens, refugees displaced by the war and its aftermath. Mostly males at first, wives and children following.

The white immigrants fitted easily into the economic and social mainstream. The blacks were ostracized, exploited and rejected. Inevitably many of them found the social pressures unbearable and sought help from the Welfare Department. Here they discovered new pressures from operatives who claimed they did not and could not understand the black immigrants and were quite helpless to aid them. It was believed by the Council that they needed, within the department, someone black, with a knowledge of the host society and generally an understanding of the conditions from which many of the blacks emigrated. When approached, I argued that my knowledge of such conditions was very sketchy and limited to my own country. Furthermore, while at home, I was either untouched by many of the prevailing social pressures or too young and pre-occupied with my own ambitions to care. The Council brushed aside my reservations, asserting that my demonstrated ability as a teacher was recommendation enough.

Perhaps I was willing to be persuaded. Undoubtedly I was flattered at their recognition of my ability, even though it was not the level of recognition for which I'd studied and striven. I accepted the job and was given an office in central London with considerable freedom to operate within the Council's wide-ranging area of influence. I was expected to visit the many area offices and consult with the welfare officers about general matters affecting black welfare recipients or particular instances which posed special problems.

Before long I began to have grave doubts about ever being really useful in the Welfare Department. Not because of the work or the problems presented to me. They were, every one of them, merely human problems. People had left their familiar situation of hopelessness and despair for an unfamiliar situation which promised betterment. These were not seekers after the proverbial pot of gold. These were men obsessed with the need to work, to earn, that they and those who depended on them might live with dignity. They had heard of available employment at good wages and had come to find it. With and without skills. Some of them at considerable personal sacrifice, so great was their hope, so persistent their faith in a brighter tomorrow.

In Britain the new conditions severely tested that faith. Long working hours for people generally unaccustomed to regular employment. An abrupt transition, to the severe pace of working in a factory or on a building site, for people hitherto conditioned by a more casual approach to labor. Time clocks. Traveling on buses and Underground trains. Accommodating themselves to the unfamiliar pounds, shillings and pence of the British currency, to new eating habits, to summer heat and winter cold, to an unfamiliar language or a familiar language used unfamiliarly and to the rigors of being semiliterate or illiterate in a highly literate society. All this and housing, too.

The black immigrants were needed. As every soldier or sailor or airman had been needed during the war, so every pair of strong arms was needed during reconstruction. Englishmen abandoned unskilled or semiskilled jobs with the public utilities for the bigger pay packets available in the booming industries. The immigrants, especially the blacks, filled these vacancies. In the hospitals. On the buses and trams. As postmen. As garbage collectors and street cleaners. As unskilled building laborers. Before long it became apparent that these utilities could hardly function without them. They were needed for the valuable services they provided, but their presence was resented. If, like genies, they could have been summoned to perform those services, then conveniently commanded to return to invisible bottles, all would have been well.

Being human, they needed to be housed.

Every kind of discriminatory device was used to restrict them to the most deplorable and dilapidated sections of the towns and cities in which they worked. Those who aspired to ownership and saved and scrimped to achieve it were barred from entry to better housing by suddenly inflated prices or by prescriptive covenants. Their difficulties and frustrations increased.

Being men they needed women.

Some married women of the host community and so invited further tensions. Others sent for wives and children to join them, inevitably imposing further strain on the inadequate housing. In these desperate conditions some broke under the cumulative pressures, and became prone to the social evils which generally overtake people in similar circumstances. Black and white.

The British, including the welfare officers, were discovering that these immigrants needed food and they needed shelter, they needed warmth against the cold and they needed to be clothed. They bred children and these children needed to be schooled. The British were just not prepared for all this. These same British, who had colonized nearly three-quarters of the world, and had acquired a reputation for tolerance and justice in those colonial territories, were suddenly finding that this reputation was being tested where they least welcomed such testing—on their own doorstep.

They were coming out of the experience very badly, because they saw themselves as wonderful and great and superior people, and they did not like the experience of living so close to inferior people. The results of their policy of colonization had merely rendered them even more secure in their sense of superiority. In the colonies they governed inferiors and they were not yet ready to have those inferiors as their neighbors, expecting or demanding any kind of equality with them.

So there I was, trying to be the middle man between black-immigrant workers who, like all humans, were sensitive people and immediately responsive to social stimuli, including rejection and hatred and discourtesy, and the host community which needed their work but resented their presence. I, who had gone that route, having to talk to white authority about how to behave to these immigrant blacks and finding that the whole thing was a fantastic charade. The prerequisite for decent behavior was that white officials see the immigrant workers simply as other human beings with the same needs, the same inclinations, the same hopes, the same fears. And they weren't ready to do this. Inevitably, all that I could possibly experience in that situation was frustration.

Every time I had to investigate the case of an immigrant, I knew I could never be objective enough to divorce myself from that circumstance. I tried, I tried desperately to be objective, but found that it was impossible. I was advised by the white authority not to become involved, but how in hell could I not be involved with myself? I was me and all those black people reminded me that they too were me, so how could I not be involved with them?

The children suffered most. Many were abandoned to become charges of the welfare state and those who manned that particular area of its activities, the child-welfare officers.

Whites who needed their help were cases. They were understandable. They could talk with them, empathize with them, argue with them and help them. Even the repeaters, the ones incapable of holding a job or managing their own affairs, merited sympathetic consideration. Blacks, on the other hand, were problems. They were approached as problems, generally getting short shrift from the welfare officers, who viewed them through the glass of conditioned contempt, darkly. This was the situation. I entered it believing that I could sway some attitudes. I met resistance at every step. From my white colleagues who resented an "untrained, inexperienced" person working among them with such a wide mandate. They resisted my suggestions and recommendations. They *knew* about blacks and how they should be handled.

At first, I was no more welcome to the blacks. Their experiences with welfare officers had, for the most part, embittered them. They mistrusted them. My appearance did not excite or encourage them. I was just another one of those who invaded their privacy and treated them with contempt. So I had a black skin. So what?

I had to prove myself to them. Suspecting and expecting betrayal from one of their own kind, they made my work extremely difficult. Deliberately they would be late for appointments at my office, or be absent from home when I was expected to call. At interviews they would be sullen and uncooperative, watching me, waiting for me to do or say the thing which would justify their distrust of me.

I had been that road before. I'd not been driven to such straits that I needed welfare assistance, but it had been close. Damned close. So I understood what motivated these attitudes. No matter what they did or said, I insisted on treating them with courtesy and respect. Without attempting to be too pally. I made it clear to them that my business was to serve them in whatever way I could within the Council's regulations. I was paid to do that. I was not granting them favors by being available to them. Gradually, very gradually, it worked. Word got around. The blacks would come to my office and insist on seeing me, and that, too, irritated my colleagues.

Part of the program was to locate foster parents for the children in the Council's care. Finding homes for white children was difficult. For black children, impossible. Or so they claimed. The established technique involved matching the children to the prospective parent. This "matching" was at the pleasure and discretion of the welfare officers who believed that the primary principle to be followed was "match the color." White to white. Black to black. Naturally, anything not white was black.

In these circumstances no prospective black foster parents appeared. None were discovered. The black children would languish in the Council's homes, year after year, until they were old enough to fend for themselves. Unless I could work a miracle or two and conjure up some black foster parents.

I worked no magic, but I was lucky. In time I found some foster parents. White ones. By the simple expedient of offering them what seemed to be a reasonable amount of money to care for a child or children in their own homes. Some of these white women, housewives anxious to earn to supplement their husband's wages, were willing to undertake just such a job. Some had a child or children of their own. They understood the needs of children and felt equipped to deal with them. The idea of working with a familiar situation in a familiar environment appealed to them. They'd be supervised from a fair distance to ensure that the job was well done. Every care would be taken in checking out the applicants.

It appealed to me. The prospect of the black children growing up in ordinary homes, even with unusual parents and peers. If certain frictions arose, well, they happened in any family. I thought of my own relationship with the Rowlands, Mum and Dad. It had not always run smoothly, but it worked. Perhaps there were other Mrs. Rowlands waiting to emerge.

I ran into difficulties right from the start. From my colleagues. From the welfare hierarchy. Everyone was sure my plan would never work. They distrusted the idea of placing a black child with white adults. If the white adults were enthusiastic, they saw it as evidence of the attraction of the exotic. The wish of the white woman to have a living black doll. "What happens when the child grows up to puberty and beyond? If the child is a girl, what happens when she is old enough for boy friends? Where will she find them if all the people she knows are white? And suppose the child is a boy? Imagine an adolescent black boy in a white household. What if there are young girls in the household?" On and on. The number and variety of hypotheses they threw at me, each one intended to make me see the awful enormity of the thing I was suggesting.

They were not prejudiced. Of that they were absolutely certain. But they had to be realistic. On and on they argued. To me. Particularly boosting the terrifying specter of the black adolescent male on nightly rampage, deflowering his foster sisters. Saying this to me, as if I had myself somehow become emasculated, safe, beyond any identification with the thoughts which terrified them.

Then there was the money. The Council had established certain definite regulations governing payments to foster parents. People should not be encouraged to become foster parents in the hope of financial gain. Altruism was the only acceptable motive. Any departure from the regulations would open the door to unscrupulous people who would take advantage of such a situation. In rebuttal I argued that the Council paid staff to care for the children in the Council's home. Such staff were salaried. The cost per child in residence in one of those homes was very high, and rising each year. Nonaltruistic foster mothers would cost less and the children would benefit far more.

In the two years I worked in the Welfare Department I was able to place only four children with foster parents. No black foster parents. The few black women were usually housewives, themselves burdened with large broods. Four black children in four white homes. Four children in four homes. It worked for them. It might have worked for others but the weight of resistant bureaucracy defeated me. That and the quietly insistent prejudices of my white colleagues. They were, in the main, fine people, each believing in the rightness of his or her opinions. Each was sure that his rejection of the idea I presented was only in the interests of the child. Black children should be with their own kind. Any interference with the natural order of things would only produce greater problems. So they said.

Each day on the job was loaded with frustrations for me. I'd been seconded to the department on the assumption that my advice would be helpful. Each time I advised or suggested ways and means of treating matters relating to the blacks, I was confronted with rules and regulations to the contrary. It did not help them when I argued that those rules predated the circumstances we faced, and that those rules had not anticipated the national attitude to blacks.

I bore it as long as I could. Perhaps I was unable to separate myself from the other, less fortunate blacks. Perhaps the memory of my own rejection was too clear in my mind. The conduct of my white colleagues to black clients was not dissimilar from the conduct of the personnel officers and interview-board members I had encountered. These black clients were in the same dependent position as I had been. Needing reassurance and help. Receiving little more than poorly disguised contempt. Sometimes I'd overhear colleagues discussing one of their black "cases" in a way which would bring the anger boiling up inside me.

"How was it today?" one would ask another.

"Damned awful. Popped over to Brixton to take a look at the Smith case. Think I'll have to recommend that those four children be taken from that woman and put into the Council's care. God, the mess! Those blacks live like animals."

"How old are the kids?"

"Five, four, three and a ten-month-old baby. The mother claims she's too sick to work, but she evidently has no difficulty rolling over. People like that ought to be sterilized."

"Or educated."

"Educated? Those blacks? All their brains are between their legs." I ended it suddenly.

Merely for a change in the dull, daily routine of riding the Underground to work all the way, I left the train at Mile End Station and caught a bus for the rest of the journey, climbing to the upper deck. It was crowded but I spotted a vacant aisle seat near the front and squeezed my way up there. When I'd settled myself I noticed that my neighbor was black. His face, under a wide-brimmed hat, was turned towards the window as if he were deeply interested in the drab sameness of the scene which flitted by. I said, "Hi, there." He turned, regarded me gravely for a moment, then, "Hi, man." He was thin, and very young, the scraggly beard on his chin notwithstanding. No more than eighteen, I thought. Thin, evidently underfed. The thick clothing loose around a wiry neck and wrists. Long bony fingers.

"Working around here?" he asked me.

"Yes," I replied. "On the other side of the river. Near Brixton."

"You're lucky. I'm going to the Labour Exchange, but I know it's a fucking waste of time. Yet if I don't go, it's always the day somebody says they've been taking on men."

"Been out of work long?" From me.

"Yes. Eighteen weeks. Feels like a hundred years. Every day I go down there and it's the same thing. Nothing today. If I don't feel well and I miss a day, they say I should have been there. They needed some men. I'll sure as hell hear it again today. Nothing. All the time you see the notices up. Jobs. All kinds of jobs. Skilled and unskilled jobs. And every one with the fucking N.C. at the end of it. The white men don't want those jobs, but still they put the fucking N.C. on them." His voice became flat with hate. "You know what I think, pal? I think they just make up those cards and put the N.C. on them just to show us they think we're shit. That's what it is. Just to laugh in their guts when they see us come in and read those notices. They want us to know they don't want us. Christ! I'd like to take all those fucking notices and stuff them right up their arse."

As he spoke I watched his face, and the stark, bitter hatred etched deeply in each line of it. At first he had seemed nondescript in the black-dyed ex-army greatcoat and the wide-brimmed hat pulled low over his face. Now his eyes were narrowed and glinting, his features squeezed into a sharp, vindictive mask. He was in pain, deep down in his spirit. Caught off guard by his outburst, I could find no words to say to him. Nothing strong enough, honest enough or meaningful enough to reach his hurt or touch the simple rightness of his hatred. All I could do was listen and understand, because I had been that way. I had walked that road.

He wanted to work, to preserve his dignity and self-respect. But at each step he was thwarted by the very people who claimed that blacks were idle, blacks were lazy, blacks preferred to batten on welfare assistance rather than seek employment. I knew what N.C meant. No colored wanted. Two little letters at the end of an advertisement and yet they could engender such cumulative bitterness and anger. The greatest irony lay in the fact that the Labour Exchanges are government offices of the Ministry of Labour. Under the auspices of the highest authority that young black man was being pressured until all he had left was his hate.

Through nine years of teaching and nearly two years in the

Welfare Department I had reached the point of nearly convincing myself that I had put every vestige of bitterness and racial hatred behind me. And yet, after little more than two minutes with that young man, a complete stranger, nameless to me, I felt it all again inside me, insistently alive, clamoring for attention. Looking around, it was immediately obvious that he and I, the only two blacks on that upper deck of the bus, were, to the other passengers, two black faces. Equally despised. Equally unacceptable. If I went with him to the Labour Exchange, I'd very likely receive the same treatment. N.C.

Later that day I prepared my resignation and took it personally to the director of the department. After reading it, he said, "I hope you're not serious about this, Mr. Braithwaite."

"Yes, Sir, quite serious."

"But we're depending on you. We need you, Braithwaite."

"I really don't think so, Sir."

"Come, come. Be sensible. No need to be precipitate. After all where do you think you'll find another . . . " Stopping suddenly as if aware that he'd said too much. I left him there, with my resignation in his hand, and the spectacles pushed up on his forehead like extra blind eyes.

"Yes. I quit teaching," I told him.

"To write full time?"

"Let's say to write a book."

"What sort of book? What did you write about?" Interested now. Inching a little nearer. Not touching. Just a little nearer.

"About myself."

"About yourself? An autobiography? At your age? What on

earth made you think of that?" Pulling off the glasses to squint at me. Hell, the invisible presence no longer bothered him. At this rate he might get near enough to touch.

"Just one of those things," I told him. Leaving him there, on the outside, while I continued backtracking down the long corridors of memory.

Writing that first book was as much an accident as my entry into teaching. Unexpected. Unplanned. It happened about a year after I was seconded to the Welfare Department.

I was enjoying a short holiday during the summer, mostly sitting around the house or otherwise idling the days away. One morning I decided to give my room and its contents a thorough cleanup. In this mood I collected much of the trivia which over the years had attached to me, including the pile of notebooks, and hauled all of it into the backyard, intending to make a bonfire.

The weather was lovely and I was in no hurry. Comfortably stretched under an apple tree I began leafing through those note-books, that laboriously compiled record of nine years of teaching. From this distance of experience and hindsight it was sobering to realize how stupid I had been. The record stared me in the face, mocking me. I had written about my pupils, arguing with myself that I was observing them, looking squarely at them, learning about them. Reading it now it seemed that I had been looking down on them from the lofty height of my own background, education, my snobbish preoccupation with clothes and my supercilious con-tempt for their speech. I'd recorded the things they said and the way they said them, with tiny special notations on the way some words took an awful beating:

"This bleeder sitting near me in the flicks cracking his bleed-
ing peanuts I couldn't hear what the bleeding bloke is saying
on the bleeding screen," all in one breath. Boys and girls.

BOY: "Hey, saw your sister with a bloke down by the pub
last night."

GIRL: "Okay, so you got two bleeding eyes."

BOY: "He her new steady?" Laughing.

GIRL: "Mind your own bleeding business." Angry.

BOY: "What's happened to that other bloke she had? In
the clink?"

GIRL: "Fuck you, Denham."

BOY: "What, now? Yes, please."

GIRL: "Oh, get stuffed."

Neither caring about being overheard.

Reading and seeing them in the pages. Pamela and Pat and Angie and Sheila. And the others. The words coloring my opinion of them, my attitude toward them. Such words came out of tarts. The words and the bright, knowing eyes. They knew all about it. God, I wondered how I must have seemed to them! Have sounded to them! Venting on them the pent-up anger and spite from a hundred rejections. Pouring my scorn and contempt through the niceties of carefully correct speech and a determined refusal to be prodded into anger by anything they could do or say. Seeing them as too far beneath me to warrant my anger. Learning later to see beyond the dress and words and the aggressive posture to the decency and strength and beauty. Learning about myself through learning about them. Growing with them.

Where were they now, nine years later? Some kept in touch.

Pamela. Beautiful, red-haired, statuesque Pamela. Modeling clothes for several smart West End shops, and sharing a flat with her mother in Hampstead. Denham. Sergeant P. Denham, now with Her Majesty's Army of the Rhine. Still determined to be his own boss one day. No longer limiting his ambition to owning a "fruit barrow." Now it would be a greengrocer's shop, one of his letters had informed me: " . . . big, fancy shop with only the best stuff at fancy prices for toffs, like you . . . ." Seales, in the final phase of apprenticeship with English Electric, safely through his City and Guilds examinations. The one, long, informative letter ending, " . . . Pam and me are planning to get married the end of next month. Nothing big. Just her parents and me Dad. So I'm not inviting you, just want you to know . . . " I wondered about Pam. Was she white, as his mother had been? Guess so. Tich Jackson, tiny, irrepressible Tich, a page at the Savoy Hotel. Marie and Betty married to twin brothers. I'd received the sliver of wedding cake, carefully wrapped in the tiny, decorated box, but inedibly hard after three days in the post. Others I heard about. Meeting Moira Joseph accidentally on the Underground, prim in her white nurse's uniform and dark blue cape. Her pride in showing the medal for heading her graduating class. Her gay chatter and the faint, pleasing, antiseptic odor.

Laughing together over old times. Sir, you remember when . . . Still "Sir." Yes, I remembered when . . . That pompous speaker from, was it the Ministry of Information? He'd come to address the class on "Life in Ceylon." Large and tight-packed in a heavy woolen suit. Evidently a man who made concessions to no one, not even the summer weather. Speaking of the "fine Singhalese people" as if he personally owned them. Boring the hell out of my class and making me nervous as I wondered what stunt they might dream up to end the boredom. A dragonfly had saved the day. From whatever distant pond, it had fluttered and found its way up between the space where the two halves of the hinged window never quite met, and now buzzed and banged itself up and down the panes striving to be free once again. The speaker droned on. The pale sun filtered through the grimy window to stir brief reflections from the insect's iridescent wings. One by one the class nudged each other's attention to the little drama above and behind the speaker's head. Ripples of concern as the dragonfly would move to within half an inch of freedom, then abruptly turn to bang itself stupidly up and down the window. Again it rested on the space, the doorway to freedom, and again veered off to continue the unequal struggle with the panes. The speaker was in full flight, perhaps seeing all those faces interestedly focused in his direction. Again the insect lit on the lower window. This time instinct and accident merged and in a flash it was out and away. A soft sigh from the class, timed to perfection with the speaker's final words. He later expressed his pleasure at the rapt attention he received.

Reading it and laughing now as Moira and I had laughed, recalling the time and the happening and those of her former schoolmates whom she occasionally saw or heard about. It was gratifying to believe that I had played some small part by encouraging her towards earlier achievement. Mum coming out to ask what was causing me such amusement. I read to her at random from the pages.

She had heard it all long ago when it had happened and she shared the reminiscing. Soon Dad joined us and together we talked of those days of struggle, their charity omitting any reference to my own conduct which must have been very painful to them. Mum asked why I had brought the notebooks outdoors and was alarmed to hear that I intended burning them.

"Why don't you put it all together into a book?" she asked.

The idea had never occurred to me. Now it startled me. I argued that I could never write a book. People who wrote books would have studied literature and understood the techniques of writing. I love reading. Every time I see a book I am conscious of the monumental task involved in putting all those words together to make interesting and sometimes exciting sense. I could not see myself doing it. However, she argued, and finally with Dad's support took the notebooks back indoors.

Hardly a day would pass but she would find some way of reminding me that instead of just sitting around, I could be working on the book. To my surprise, and somewhat to my dismay, Dad joined her. So one day I thought to myself, "Okay, if she wants a book she will get a book." With the little money I had, I bought some typing paper and hired a second-hand typewriter. I put a collapsible bridge table under the apple tree in the back yard, took the notebooks and beginning from page one of book number one, typed what I had written down. All of it.

Whenever I came to an interruption in the record, I could easily from memory introduce something which bridged the gap. It was going very nicely, when, talking to Mum one day she remarked, "That's not how you began. Why did you go into teaching in the first place?" She knew the story just as well as I did. I reminded her. She said, "Don't tell me. Put it down." I thought to myself, "Why should I put it down in the middle?" So I got some more paper and started all over again, beginning now with why I went into teaching and then taking the story on from there. When it was finished, I had quite a pile of typescript.

Altogether I took about three weeks to do the transcription. Completed, I took the pages to a local printer and asked him to staple them together for me. He even put some pasteboard on either side. Just to hold the thing together. I thought to myself, "Mum wanted a book so I'm going to give her a book." I needed a title. At the end I had related how the kids had made me a gift, a large box of cigarettes. They had gone to W. D. and H. O. Wills in London and ordered five hundred cigarettes, each one with my initials E.R.B. on it, packed in a beautiful presentation box. On the wrapping of the box, they had stuck a piece of paper and written on it, TO SIR, WITH LOVE. Underneath this each one of them had signed his or her name. Looking at this I thought, "Can I call it *To Sir, With Love?* Oh, well, it's just for Mum. She'll understand." So I entitled it *To Sir, With Love* by E. R. Braithwaite.

The following morning at breakfast time I put it on her plate. She looked at it and said, "So you see, there it is. Now do something with it." "Like what?" I asked and she said, "I don't know. Just do something with it." Just to please her I took it with me to ask the advice of the local librarian. He suggested that I let him read it. Two days later I visited him again. He said, "I think it has something, but I'm not sure if I feel that way because I know you or because of some quality the thing has. Why don't you take it to an agent, somebody who doesn't know you, and could offer a real opinion?" I told him I couldn't afford to employ an agent. "It won't cost you anything," he said. "If the agent thinks it's good he will try and place it for you and take a percentage. If he doesn't, he'll tell you so and that's all there is to it." From one of his shelves he reached down *The Writers' and Artists' Yearbook.* We looked through this to find an agent, deciding on the firm of Peam, Pollinger, and Higham, established years and years ago in Dean Street. Soho. London.

The following day I took the manuscript to the London agent.

Everything about the place, the pretentious doorway, narrow lobby and rickety stairs upward to the receptionist's cubicle, suggested age. I could easily imagine Charles Dickens coming to this place. It was intended for important, established authors. What was I doing here? The receptionist seemed out of place. Too young, too attractive, but when she spoke to me neither her voice nor her manner was encouraging. Looking me quickly up and down as if capable of determining my literary pretensions, all in one comprehensive glance, she said, "Yes."

I was immediately filled with the wildest urge to say something like, "But you haven't yet heard my proposition," and as quickly decided against it. It was amusing to recall how diffident I had been in approaching these people during my job-hunting days, when I had believed that they were part of the hiring process and I should be particularly courteous to them. Actually, they often proved to be no less contemptuous than their employers and may have even enjoyed the sight of my diffidence and unease. Now I said to this one, "I have a manuscript here which I would like to have considered with a view to possible publication." Cool. Even casual. Laying the thick book on her desk. Those level gray eyes studied me, as if the mind behind them was now testing my voice for quality. Abruptly swinging the eyes away she let them traverse the shelves which lined the three sides of the reception area. Most of these shelves bulged with fat packages, some held together with string. When the gray eyes returned to me the neat eyebrows were lifted quizzically. I got the message and reached for the manuscript but her quick, manicured hand was there ahead of me, spread-fingered.

"What's your hurry?" No trace of a smile.

"Well, if you don't think . . . "

She turned the manuscript around the better to read the title and author's name. Again the eyebrows going up. Was it the name or the title?

"If you will write your address and telephone number somewhere on the top," pointing with a smooth, shiny finger, "I will send it in to our editorial section."

"Then what?" I asked.

"I suppose it will eventually be sent to one of our readers for an opinion." Making the word eventually sound like forever.

"How long will that take?"

"I'm afraid I couldn't answer that. A few months, perhaps. Our readers are all very busy at the moment. Incidentally, who sent you to us?"

"My local librarian."

"Do we represent him?"

"No. We chose your agency from the list in the *Year Book*. He and I." Making it sound quite random. Anything to take her down a peg or two. Continuing with, "Well, shall I check with you in a week or two?"

"No. That won't be necessary. We have your address and we'll write to you when we have the reader's report."

Turning away to indicate the end of the conversation. I was tempted to pick up the manuscript anyway, but I'd come this far. Okay. Why let myself be so easily irritated? After all, she'd not said or done anything really discourteous. Perhaps that abrasive manner was normal with her. Wouldn't it shake her up if the reader, whoever he or she was, came up with a favorable report?

From Dean Street I cut across Frith Street to take the bus at Shaftesbury Avenue. Going in the same direction and a few yards ahead of me was a very shapely young woman perched high on spindly heels which emphasized the sway of her hips. A large, shiny black handbag hung from the crook of her left elbow. From time to time she brought the fingers of her right hand to pat into place the mass of blond ringlets piled on her head and about the nape of her neck. Something about her was oddly familiar, even as I argued with myself that I could not possibly know her. I admired the ease with which she balanced herself on the high, shiny heels, each foot placed primly in front of the other. Either I had hurried or her pace had slowed, but soon I was alongside, glancing sideways to see the face that went with the rest of her. At the same time she glanced across at me.

She had been one of my students, a member of my first class. The well-developed blonde with the large green eyes whom the others nicknamed Droopy because foundation supports always seemed inadequate to the task required of them. Quick-willed and friendly, she treated her peers, however, with something approaching disdain, as if they were far too gauche for her. It was rumored that after school hours and at weekends she frequented some of the local workingmen's clubs. Now here she was.

I saw the recognition in her eyes. They remained on me for a moment, cool, unbothered. One shoulder came up in a shrug as she adjusted the strap of her handbag. The face was still youthfully lovely, the figure still voluptuous. Unhurriedly she turned away and crossed the street to the other pavement.

At home I told Mum and Dad how I had fared at the agency, and of my wordless encounter with my ex-student. "Wish her luck," Mum advised. "After all, in this world it takes all kinds." That, and even the likely fate of the manuscript were forgotten that night and the following morning, as I was once again lazily stretched in the sun under the apple tree.

Sometime around mid-morning Mum called me with the news that there was a telephone call for me. It was the agency. Peam, Pollinger, and Higham. Someone who identified himself as an editor was calling to ask whether I could come to London and lunch with him. That very day. He wanted to talk to me about my manuscript, *To Sir, With Love.*

I was stunned. The receptionist had said they'd be in touch in, maybe, weeks. Perhaps months. Yet here was this person calling already. I assured him I'd be there, hung up and shouted the news to Mum. She hurried from the kitchen, wiping her hands on her apron, concern written large on her face. Not understanding what I'd shouted down the passage and through the kitchen door. Eventually coherent, I explained.

"Oh, that!" she said. "Good for them. Well, go on upstairs and get yourself ready." Making one of the most important moments in my life seem quite ordinary.

On the way to London the initial euphoria quickly evaporated as I remembered that the man had not said much. He'd not said whether or not he liked the book. Anyway, he wanted to talk with me about it. That was a good sign. Maybe he wanted to advise me about it, how it should better be written. Editors knew about those things. I'd read somewhere that if they liked a part of a book, they would help the author to reorganize the rest upward to the level of that part. If they didn't like it they'd not be calling me, so perhaps it had a chance.

This time the receptionist was quite friendly. She even remembered my name. Mr. Bellamy was expecting me. She telephoned him to let him know I'd arrived, and in a few minutes he appeared. A slim, balding but youthful man who greeted me warmly and led me upstairs to the cubbyhole of an office he shared with several hundred books, mostly on bookshelves, but others on his desk, on the radiator, on the window-sill and even in a neat pile on the floor. He had to clear some from the armchair near his desk before I could sit down.

"Please excuse me a moment," he said. "Just have to get through a few little matters then we can pop out and have a spot of lunch." Quickly busying himself with telephone calls and several papers which a secretary brought in to him. I sat there in a frenzy of impatience, striving to appear casual.

After what seemed like an hour, but may have been only fifteen or twenty minutes, he was ready. Together we went to a pub in Soho where he was evidently well known. After we'd found a table he pointed out several nationally known personalities, actors, writers, a member of Parliament. We ordered *apéritifs* and he spent an awfully long time with the menu, choosing for both of us. At that moment my interest in food was negligible, in inverse ratio to my impatience, but I was determined to let him be the first to open the conversation. He chatted amiably about food and publishing and Soho and theatre and everything except what I was so anxious to hear. Our meal was served, with two large tankards of mild beer. I hardly tasted either, marveling at the man and his singleminded occupation with what was before him. Eventually that was done and the dishes taken away. Then the performance of choosing the right brandy with coffee. Demitasse.

Finally he leaned back and said, "I suppose you're wondering about your manuscript and what this is all about."

I could only nod at him. No words.

"Well," he continued, "first of all, let me tell you that I like it. There are one or two little details which need attention. Tiny ones, mark you, but they should present no difficulties."

Still no words from me. My mind, my spirit, everything except my body, seemed to be floating high overhead. Carefully pulling up the sleeves of his jacket for comfort, he rested both elbows on the table, cupped his narrow face in his palms and, smiling, said, "Guess you're wondering how we've got to it so quickly." Reading into those words all the questions darting about in my confused mind.

"I am.

"Well, it's like this," he said, and unfolded the following story.

He lived in one of the towns of suburban Middlesex, and, normally, commuted between home and office by car. The day before, however, he and his wife had arranged to meet friends in London for dinner and the theatre. To best accommodate this arrangement, he'd traveled to London by train, leaving the car for his wife who would drive in early that evening and collect him from his office. At about four o'clock his wife had telephoned him complaining of illness and suggesting that the evening's party be postponed for another time.

On his way past the receptionist that evening he casually asked if there was anything around which he might read on the journey home. He'd forgotten to pick up one of the books in his office. Just as casually she showed him my manuscript, with the remark that that was all that had come in that day. Reluctantly he took it, although intrigued by the title. Once settled in the train he began reading.

"It was the first time since my schooldays that I'd ever sat in a train and been taken past my destination," he told me. "So absorbed I became in the book."

After dinner that evening he finished it.

"I'm impressed by the way you write," he said. "Your style. The way you make your characters live."

"They're all alive," I told him.

"You mean it's all true?"

"Exactly. Just as it happened."

"What about names of people?"

"Everything."

"Then we have a few problems," he said. "A publisher would want to ensure that there's no likelihood of anyone starting libel action. And the language of some of the students is a bit ripe, wouldn't you agree?"

"It's factual."

"I'm not doubting that. I'm merely mentioning some of the difficulties which may arise. Anyway, all that's for the publishers to decide. I have two of them in mind. The Bodley Head and Secker and Warburg. I'd suggest we send it first to The Bodley Head. They're a bit prestigious and stuffy, but I've an idea they might like it."

"Whatever you say." I meant that. Everything was happening so quickly, I was hardly hearing the details for the turmoil of happiness in my head. I'd written a book and it would be published. I was impatient to get home with the news.

"Was it published?" my companion was asking.

"Oh, yes." Smiling with the memory of it. The pleasure of it.

"In England or here in the U.S.?"

"Both." Volunteering nothing.

"What's the title of it? Perhaps I know it. My wife and I do a lot of reading."

"*To Sir, With Love.*" It took a second or two to sink in. His mouth opened in a soundless "O." He removed the glasses to peer at me, as if he'd not yet fully remarked my features.

"'*To Sir, With Love!*' I know that. Not the book. I haven't read the book. But the movie. They made a movie of it, didn't they? With

Sidney Poitier. I saw the movie. We all saw it. At the local play-house. The whole family. Autobiographical, did you say?"

"Yes."

"And that's the school you were talking about? And the students?"

"As near as the movie people could get to it."

"Wow! Yes. I remember. My wife and the kids wept through most of that film. Driving home we were talking about it. Remember my wife saying that teacher must have been quite a man. But she couldn't understand how he could keep his cool like that all the time. She said she'd have blown her top a thousand times over."

"Well, I did. Eventually."

"Yes. But even so, you were always so controlled. But, hell, isn't it a small world? To think we'd meet and be talking this way. Wait till I phone my wife and tell her. The kids will never believe it. I've two girls, both at high school. They read the book as part of their English course." Beaming at me. "Wow! Soon as I get to my office I'll have my secretary check the bookshops to find a copy. Now I must read it."

I tried to keep a straight face. Just listen to him! Talking of our meeting as if it had been something he'd welcomed. I noticed the transformation in him, the new element in his voice, his manner. Respect. That's what it was. Unmistakably. Not for me. Hell, no! I'd not changed one bit during the time he'd sat beside me. It was for the other things to which people like him always responded. The ability, the talent, the gift, whatever it was he now knew I possessed. All of it packaged together and labeled success. I had earlier mentioned that I wrote, but he'd taken it in his stride. No bells had rung for him then. But now it was pinpointed as something he'd seen portrayed, irrefutable evidence of success. I smiled at the thought that he'd so narrowly missed it all. He'd come so close to being put off by my black face! Now he'd have quite a story for his secretary, his wife and his children. I wondered how he'd introduce it. Perhaps, something like, "I rode into the city this morning beside a black man, and guess who it turned out to be." Or, more simply, "You'd never guess who I met this morning on the ride to New York." Oh, well!

"Best seller, wasn't it? The book, I mean."

"In England. Yes. So far I believe it has been translated into twenty-five different languages." Laying it on thickly.

"What about here, in the U.S.?"

"Oh, I think it has had some moderate success here, too. Even a literary award."

"A literary award? Which one?" Like a beagle on the scent.

"The Anisfield-Wolff Award." Casual. Quiet. Keeping it cool. Inside myself enjoying his surprise. The way he was looking at me as if I'd done a chameleon act before his very eyes. Changed myself into someone he could even be friendly with. Black skin and all. How else could he relate to the other things? The skill. The talent. The ability. One minute I had been an undesirable black, unwelcome; now I'd metamorphosed into a repository of the things he respected, perhaps strove and hungered for.

"So that was the start of your writing career?" he wanted to know.

"Not exactly."

It had not become a career. Not then. Even in spite of all the wonderful reviews and interviews and pats on the back. The thing that had frightened me was the realization that I was expected to continue writing. The publishers. My agent. The reviewers. Everyone spoke of the book as if they expected it to be the first of many. In fact, I could think of nothing else to write about. I had lived through that experience. In setting it down I had tried to recreate the circumstances as accurately as possible. Dialogue, situations, everything. Telling the story and reliving it at the same time.

However I suppose I responded to the praise and encouragement. I argued with myself that all the experts couldn't be wrong. If they said I could write, then perhaps I could. Encouraged by my agent, I wrote a few short pieces for the B.B.C. radio. On teaching. They were accepted and I read them on the air. The next step was in natural sequence. Articles for *The Times, The Observer, The Guardian* and *The Statesman.* On education, on teaching and on the plight of the black immigrant in Britain. The outsider writing from inside. Critically.

"What then? Did you try to find another job?"

"No. Another job found me."

The fees from the newspapers and broadcasting had been enough. Nothing wonderful, but altogether not much less than what I received from teaching or from the Welfare Department. Then there was the money from the publishers. An advance on royalties. A few hundred pounds but, at that time, a small fortune to me. The pieces I wrote and broadcast attracted a lot of favorable attention. Together with the wonderful publicity from my book. Letters poured in from readers of all kinds, especially teachers, nearly all of them very complimentary and encouraging. I received many invitations to address groups at colleges, schools, readers' clubs, churches, everywhere. After one such address I was introduced to a young man named Maurice Frost who told me he operated a lecture agency. When he learned that I had been asking no fees for my lectures he invited me to join his agency. I did.

So now it was writing and lecturing. Traveling around Britain, meeting and learning about others black like myself. As a welfare official I had met only those who sought help through me. Now I was meeting others. Men and women who had settled in Britain after being active in some branch of the armed services. They too had lived through experiences not unlike my own, emerging disillusioned but determined. Two dentists. A midwife. Electricians and automobile servicemen. Skilled and unskilled. Laborers and others. Employed and unemployed. Some youthful, enthusiastic and bulging with hope for better times to come. Others disillusioned, dejected and demoralized. Manchester. Birmingham. Liverpool. Cardiff. North. South. East and west.

During the time of my own desperate search for employment I'd never thought that others, black like me, were experiencing the same rejections and frustrations. I was preoccupied with myself, my pain and my need. I had no black acquaintances or intimates with whom to share or compare my daily experiences. It was me, uniquely me, against the world of whites. Then I'd found a job as teacher and, occupied with its challenges, it was still me, uniquely me, proving myself. Even when working with the Welfare Department my primary and perhaps only concern was proving myself capable, imaginatively capable, sensitively capable. Regular employment diverted my attention from hurt, rejected me to ambitious, intelligent me.

The chance encounter with the young black man on the bus affected me far more deeply than I at first realized. The depth and power of his despair were so familiar, so painfully familiar. He merely wanted a job. Any job. I'd had education, specialized training, wartime service and experience in living within the white society, but, at the final reckoning, he and I were one. We were black, and in that brief encounter, with so few words, he could say it all to me.

Now, free of departmental oversight or control, I began to look into conditions which so intimately and painfully affected him and me, and others like us. Particularly employment and housing, or should I say, the lack of both?

Wherever I went on my lecture tours I sought to make contact with blacks. It was not easy. Often my overtures to friendliness were brusquely rebuffed, but, luckily, not always. I've often wondered whether those blacks who rejected me had themselves been so often deceived and exploited that there remained no trust. For anyone. Or whether it was because of the way I was dressed, or spoke or approached them. In the comfortable years of University and the frightening excitements of war service, I'd been content with other associations, other relationships. More recent experiences had taught me to be distrustful of those relationships, and here I was now, reaching for contact with, and for acceptance among, others like myself. "My people."

Belatedly I was looking around, searching for the black faces. Needing to get close. Whenever and wherever they permitted that closeness we talked about our common experiences, our common pain. Always a recital of hurt and pain. Hate sessions. They were, for the most part, uneducated, unskilled and vulnerable. I was skilled, educated and just as vulnerable, and found it very difficult to make them understand that. The way I spoke or dressed notwithstanding. I had lived through the same hell of rejection.

The discovery of my ability to write made me want to write. As I traveled the country I became concerned to write about the conditions under which other blacks lived. I didn't think there was much I could do otherwise. Soon I met other people similarly concerned. Whites. Sociologist Richard Hauser and his wife Hephzibah Menuhin. Donald Chesworth. Many others.

I remember the circumstances of my first meeting with Richard and Hephzibah. I'd been invited to speak at a conference at the Y.W.C.A. headquarters at Tottenham Court Road. Arriving early, I was standing in the foyer outside the auditorium when two people approached me and introduced themselves. Richard and Hephzibah Hauser. We chatted idly about this and that, but soon he steered the conversation around to the problems of blacks in Britain, expressing his sympathy for their unhappy plight. I had been hearing the same kind of tiresome claptrap from so many sources recently that I responded quite angrily and not at all as he'd expected. I told him he could stuff his sympathy, or words to that effect, adding that blacks would have to learn, no matter how bitter the lesson, that their salvation would depend only on themselves. More, much more of the same.

When I'd said my piece I excused myself and was leaving, but they stopped me. Laughing. Saying they were happy to hear me say those things because they agreed with every word. They'd been hoping for just that kind of reaction. I was not convinced, but agreed to meet them again. And again. The beginning of a long and pleasant association. Their idea of helping was to encourage people needing help to be rid of that help as quickly as possible. We worked on several projects together and I learned that, very often, people in difficulty merely needed a helping hand. Not a crutch. A helping hand assumes only part of the burden, the smaller part. A crutch is made to bear most of the weight. Their simple philosophy was "help the needy to become quickly independent of you." Working with them I learned and I wrote about what I learned.

The things I wrote were finding an audience farther afield than

I realized. One day I had a letter from an international organization with headquarters in Paris. The World Veterans' Federation. The Secretary General wrote to me, expressing his interest in my work and ideas and indicating that his deputy would soon be visiting Britain and would be in touch with me. That meeting took place about a week later and resulted in my accepting a job with the Federation as their Human Rights Officer. It was interesting and challenging work.

The Federation was a collective of ex-servicemen's organizations in countries of Europe, Asia, Africa, Australia and the Americas. At the time of my appointment there was a plan to initiate several educational and social grassroots projects for ex-servicemen in some Asian and African countries. These countries were, then, within either the British or French colonial empire, and the men had been recruited to fight outside their own national borders in the colonial power's expeditionary forces.

Many had been killed. Of the survivors, some were partially or totally disabled. A few received pensions from the colonial government they'd served but these were quite inadequate for their basic needs. The national government, in most cases, was deeply involved in the pandemic struggle for independence and was loath to accept responsibility for the care and succor of nationals who had become incapacitated while serving a foreign government in a foreign country.

The grassroots projects were designed to create opportunities for the education, training and employment of ex-servicemen in ways intended to make them self-supporting. The design was related to the needs of the men within their own communities and included boat building for fishermen; poultry and pig farming for small farmers; workshops for the manufacture, fitting and training in the use of artificial limbs and other prosthetic devices which could be made from indigenous materials.

My job required me to visit the ex-servicemen's organizations, discuss with them the conditions which affected them, listen to the way in which they ordered their priorities, discuss these in the light of possible funding, then make recommendations to the Federation. At all times I sought to work in close liaison with the national government, as it was sometimes possible to assist a scheme they had already planned or undertaken.

I accepted the job in Paris because of the salary and the wonderful possibilities for working in a situation of greater personal freedom to plan and to act. I was impressed with the Secretary General's deputy. In talking to him I learned that the Federation's staff was nearly all white. I told myself I'd remember the lessons learned in Britain. I took to the new job my skills, imagination and enthusiasm. I also took all the spiritual scars collected over nearly fifteen years of life in Britain and a deep skepticism about the white man.

"A job found you? How's that?" he asked.

"I was offered a job in France."

"In France?"

"Yes. In Paris."

"Doing what?"

"Working with an international organization."

"So you went to live there."

"Naturally. Funny thing though. In spite of my difficulties in Britain I was saddened by the prospect of leaving. I had developed some very strong, intimate ties with the place and the people. After all, it was the scene of my happiest and un-happiest moments."

"Yet I suppose anyone would have jumped at the chance of working in Paris."

"There was that. And the salary offered, considerably more than I was earning then. And the prospect of extensive travel."

"What kind of travel? Within France?"

"Internationally."

"Where did you go?"

"East and West Africa. Parts of Asia. Scandinavia. Places like that."

"Must have been terribly exciting."

"Yes. It was. Very exciting."

Seeing Africa for the first time. Being with Africans. Seeing and feeling their pride in themselves, hearing of their struggles against the colonizers. Knowing that no matter how attenuated the relationship, I was a piece of the whole. Ghana. Ivory Coast, Somali, Guinea. The same earth with different markers, but I was of it. Just being there, walking on it, feeling it under me was good. Liberia, where the colonizers were themselves as black as the indigenous population, as cruel and repressive as colonizers always are, needing to establish and secure themselves, needing to exploit the land and its resources and eventually its people. Remembering that, and the other things. The ignorance, the disease, the misery. Insufficient knowledge about the land and its husbandry. Insufficient schools. Insufficient education. And a plenitude of excuses from those in control. An incident was suddenly revived, time and distance dulling the raw edges and rendering it nearly funny.

I was in Freetown, Sierra Leone, a few days before the celebrations of their independence from Britain and was invited to tea by the Governor General, Sir Maurice Dorman, an Englishman. Tea was served to the guests on the spacious lawns of his residence and we were entertained by the band of the local militia. Excerpts from the Gilbert and Sullivan operettas, a few pieces by Sousa, some Highland songs delightfully arranged and beautifully executed. Wonderful in cool open air of that African afternoon.

Later on I took an opportunity to compliment the bandmaster, an Englishman, on the band's fine performance, and then spoke with some members of the band. To my amazement I discovered that, without exception, the bandsmen, all black, could neither read nor write. All volunteer members of the militia, they had been taught to read music that they might function as a band, well-disciplined, well-practiced, and rehearsed, a delightful feature of official functions, attractive in their very colorful uniforms and glistening equipment. They all lived in the local military compound, readily available for training of any sort. But they were not taught to read and write. Those who controlled them kept them selectively functional and illiterate.

I wrote as I traveled from city to city, through town and village, across rivers and gullies, in the hinterlands, setting it down as I saw it and heard it and felt it, learning to capture the immediate impression in words. The barren hills, sunbaked into heavy stillness by day, urgent with life at night. Insect, bird and stalking creature all intent on their separate needs for survival. And the people, wearing their dignity with the nonchalance of comfortable old slippers in spite of the prevailing poverty and disease, ignorance and malnutrition.

I set it down while it was fresh in my mind's eye. Each week I sent a batch of notes to my publisher, Prentice-Hall, where they were retyped and compiled, ready for editing. Shortly after the trip was completed I was able to revise and arrange these notes into a manuscript.

Quietly the train was again in motion, but slowly. Looking around I noticed that many of the newspapers were no longer in sight. Querulous murmurings. Snatches of conversation about being late for appointment. Speculation about whatever was causing the holdup far ahead. The minutes were slipping away. Already nine o'clock and still a long way from the city. My neighbor seemed in no way perturbed.

"What was it like in Paris? Living there after England? I've visited it a couple of times since the war, but I don't know that I'd like to live there."

"Why?"

"They seem to have become more and more anti-American. You talk about contempt. Boy, they're contemptuous of everyone and everything that's not French. Didn't you experience that?"

"No. I enjoyed living there."

That was the simple truth. On arrival in Paris I'd promised myself to play everything by ear. Life in England had taught me some raw lessons. So now I was determined to expose as little as possible of myself to further bruising. That's what I'd promised myself.

The Federation had agreed to provide me with free accommodation for two weeks at a hotel within easy reach of the headquarters. During that time it was up to me to find an apartment suitable to myself. Each day I would check the newspaper advertisements on apartments for rent, particularly those within a reasonable radius from my office, asking the advice of my new colleagues as to suitability and price. I discovered that the level of rents related as much to the *arrondissement* or locality as to the size of the apartment and its furnishing.

One day I read an advertisement in the Paris edition of the American *Herald Tribune,* which interested me. It was for an apartment located in the fashionable Seventh *Arrondissement.* According to the published blurb, it was in a building within a walled courtyard containing a small garden; newly decorated and tastefully furnished; on the seventh floor with an uninterrupted view; excellent elevator service; courteous and efficient concierge. All that and about a quarter of a mile from my office. The rent was not mentioned. The telephone number was. I read it several times. The Seventh *Arrondissement.* In London that would be called a Residential area. With a capital "R." When my financial condition had suddenly improved with the publication of my book, I'd decided to move nearer to London and had read similar advertisements. I'd telephone and receive a friendly invitation to "come and see it yourself." Yet, when I arrived, the reaction to my black face had always been the same: "So sorry, but someone else has just been and taken it."

Now here it was again. Making a mental wager with myself, I dialed the number. On the third ring a voice answered. A charming woman's voice. In English, I said that I was inquiring about the apartment she'd advertised. In English, she immediately expressed her pleasure that I'd phoned, and proceeded to describe the apartment, making it sound even more attractive than had the blurb.

"And the rent, madam?" I asked.

She mentioned an amount well within the limits I had set myself. Lovely. I was about to say I was free to come and see it now, anytime, when memory warned me.

"I'd like you to know that I am black, madam," I blurted out, anxious to get it over and done with.

"I'm sorry, monsieur," she replied, "but there can be no reduction for that. *Le prix est fixe.*"

Had she been near I might have kissed her. For the first time in my life in Europe I'd heard words which told me that my color was not the main concern. I felt released, lifted. Tall. It was agreeable to have this assurance that I could live where I wanted to live. I hurried over to see the apartment. Satisfied, I rented it. I remained there the whole seven years of my stay in France.

It's interesting to reflect that she did not inquire into my background. At sight of me she did not suggest that my presence would reduce the tone or quality or value of the apartment, the building or the *arrondissement*.

"No problems?" he asked.

"No problems."

I had no doubt that the French are just as prejudiced, as discriminatory and as contemptuous as are the British, the Americans, or anyone else. As a black man I cannot afford the luxury of self-delusion. However, at no time in my seven years of living in France did their contempt crudely intervene between me and where I wanted to live, or the work I wanted to do or the people I wished to associate with. I was allowed to be myself. Feeling that wonderful warmth just by remembering.

"How long did you stay on that job?"

"Four years. In between missions I wrote another book."

"What was that about?"

"It was about my work as a welfare official in London. My experience as a teacher had shown me the value of making notes. For myself. As a way of checking my own progress and development. So, once again, from the day I began the unfamiliar job for which I had no formal training, the job of Welfare Advisor, I began taking notes. I used some of my spare time in Paris to assemble and edit those notes into a manuscript."

"How did it go? Another best seller?"

"It had a very good reception. It was published in England, Germany and Holland and later here in the United States. When I think of the thousands of books written and submitted to publishers, I am very flattered by the attention mine received."

"Deservedly so. Evidently you're an exceptional man."

"Am I?"

Christ! He was coming on. Exceptional, he called me. Funny thing is that inside myself I don't feel exceptional. There are lots like me, strong in themselves, feeling they can do things. But perhaps they're not as lucky as me. They're denied the freedom, the opportunity and the right to give expression to what they feel.

My thoughts flashed to that school I'd recently visited in Syracuse. Upstate New York. An inner-city school. Several thousand students. Nearly all black. I addressed their assembly and later spoke to some groups. I'll never forget it. Such frustration and hopelessness. Beautiful young people who should have been full of excitement and wonder and enthusiasm for life and living and doing. Unexcited about the future. Already victims of hopelessness. They, too, could be exceptional people, given half a chance.

"You made your own way, didn't you?"

"Perhaps. But the way was open. A roadblock here and there, but it was generally open. For many blacks there are no openings. They're frustrated and desperate. Like human bombs triggered and ticking away the moments to explosion."

"Aren't you using your writer's license to overdramatize the situation? Nowadays many of our youngsters are in a state of root-lessness, without direction, without anchorage. That does not make them bombs. Bums, more likely." Laughing at his own pun.

"When you say 'our youngsters' I take it you mean white young-sters. That's fine for them. They can play-act and posture to their heart's content. It's easy to reject wealth, educational opportunities, comfort, security, any of those things, if you have them or if you know they're readily available to you. You can always change your mind and return to them if your convictions desert you or if you grow tired of holding the posture. But if you never had them, nor can ever hope to have them, rejection is merely a pose. Blacks cannot even afford the pose."

Remembering my conversations with some of the members of the Syracuse faculty. Mostly white. The English teacher who showed me a piece one of the black students had turned in as part of a poetry project. It was this:

> *I wish I was a blackbird's egg*
> *High in a walnut tree.*
> *A-sitting in my little nest*
> *As rotten as could be.*
> *I wish that you would come along*
> *And stand beneath that tree*
> *So I could fall and bust myself*
> *And cover you with me.*

The teacher did not consider it funny. She, too, felt the build-up of frustration and hopelessness among the black students. She felt threatened by it. Yet she was sure she was doing her best. Her altruistic best. Daily going through the motions of teaching. She had no illusions about her role in that school. She was white. She lived in a part of town far removed from the homes of her students. In a different environment. In a different world. Isolated from them. Screened from them by zoning laws or other devices of exclusion. So how could she relate the academic abstractions to their lives? Or could she dare use her experience and way of living to illustrate her point of view? From within her own consciousness of security, how could she address herself to their insecurity and have her sincerity believed? In short, how could she teach them? What could they learn from her?

The few black teachers I met were no more effective, no more respected by the students. I saw them, heard them and talked with them. Enough of them to know that they're so trapped within the situation, they're generally no better than their white peers. But why should they be? They want to slip their chains, their encagement, and teaching is an escape hatch. Regular salary. Security of tenure. Respectability. All signs point upward, to the cleaner air. Away from the ghetto and its pervasive taint. Every man for himself. Having a thought and airing it before he could interrupt.

"Recently while I was in England there was a report of the accidental sinking of a submarine at a south coast base. Three servicemen trapped inside it. All the pathos and anxiety of rescue preparations. Finally the moment of escape. The wild bubbling of the water as air forced its way up ahead of the first man. His head breaking the surface in a shower of spray. Me thinking of the way blacks were striving to escape their encagement. Hoping to break through to social and economic freedom. But waiting for them, not the rescue parties, not cheering voices, but zoning laws. N.C. signs. There. Here. Everywhere."

"Tell me about your book, the one on welfare," he said, switching away.

"I've told you about it."

"I mean. Was it written in the same way as the first? With yourself as the central character?"

"Very much the same."

"Any film offers on that one?"

Hell, I knew he was trying to keep us off the touchy discussions. The sensitive areas. Doing it in a patient, gentlemanly way, keeping it nice and peaceful between us. Still under the *To Sir* influence? Through the window haze no more flashes of green. Buildings in the distance. The train picked up speed for a few moments, slowed again, then once more ran free.

"Do you mind if I ask you a personal question?" The tone of his voice hinting he was sure I wouldn't mind. Not now. Not with him in my corner among the *To Sir* fans.

"I'll know the answer to that after you've asked the question. Go ahead."

"Well, it's something I've heard about, but from sources which are not necessarily reliable. It's about the social life in France. Although I visited Paris a few times, I had no opportunity to discover much of what was going on. Tell me. Is it really as free and easy as some people would have us believe? I mean, for a person like yourself. A black person?"

Trying to make his question as acceptable as possible. Circling around. I immediately knew what he wanted to ask but couldn't.

It stuck in his guts. The irritation began to rumble in mine. Okay. Let's play with it.

"What do you mean by social life? Cocktail parties? Theatres? Luncheons? Dinners?"

"Yes, but more than that. Social contact. Associations. Even friendships."

"Oh, there were all of those. Among the colleagues with whom I worked. Neighbors. Eventually one made acquaintances, and some of these developed into friendships. The usual." He'd have to spell it out, the thing he had in his mind. He'd get no help from me.

"I was thinking. Bearing in mind your experiences in Britain. You were a black man in a white society. If I may say so, you're an attractive man. You'd need more than mere acquaintanceships. Or even, just friendships."

"In what way?" Keeping him on the line.

"I'm thinking of personal relationships. With women." Giving me his buddy-buddy smile.

"What about them?"

"You spoke of white contempt for blacks. Were the white women equally contemptuous? If one accepted that it was a general thing, would you say it was also a personal thing?" Circling. Clearly circling around it.

"Are you asking me if I slept with white women?" I wanted to pin the bastard down. When he said I was an attractive man he meant that I was attractive to women. Perhaps, in his mind. French women, being alien, foreign and distant, might respond to my attractiveness. An attractive, healthy man would need the intimate association of women wherever he was. Wherever he lived. Would he dare bring the question nearer home? Or did he think of

American white women as unattainable to such as myself? Christ, he must be blind!

"I'm asking if the contempt and exclusion you've been talking about prevented any deep personal relationships." Reddening a bit. Just a touch of asperity.

"No. Anyway, that's one of the absurdities of prejudice. It can always find excuses for its own default."

The red quickly spread upwards around his neck to involve his ears. Matching the edge in his voice. Hell, I'd got under the cool shell.

"Aren't you being very selective about absurdities? If you could occasionally be wrong about a personal relationship, couldn't you be equally wrong about more general attitudes?" Bravo! He'd neatly side-stepped further talk about women. I'd provided him with an exit line and he'd gobbled it up. Bright.

"Look here," I replied, "I think you're missing something. White contempt is not a matter for speculation by me. It's there all around. Observable. Demonstrable. Here. Rhodesia. England. South Africa. Germany. Russia. Gooks. Chinks. Niggers. It's there all around. Wherever I look. Wherever I go. I don't need to search or examine. Remember that proverb, 'Beware of Greeks who come bearing gifts'? To every black a friendly white is a Greek bearing gifts. Out of character. So caution dictates that we check lest it be another example of the Trojan horse."

"That's a bit arrogant, isn't it? As if you expect the overtures of friendship to come from one direction only. Always. And you scornfully set yourself up, to accept or reject."

"Perhaps." Not wanting to continue with it. Let him think whatever he wished.

"Did you meet other blacks in Paris?" he asked, again slipping away with that disarming boyish grin. Maybe this was all part of the technique of public relations. Keep smiling to keep the customers happy. The boyish, skin-deep smile.

"Yes. I met many blacks in Paris. Residents. Students. Diplomats. Painters. Poets. Models. Entertainers. Street cleaners, dustmen. Prostitutes. They're all there."

"That's fine, but what I want to know is, did you seek their company exclusively from the company of whites? Or were you able to forget your experiences in England on arrival in France? There's a reason for my asking this. Over here one hears of blacks claiming that they've given up being reasonable with whites or even talking with them. They want to be separate. Separate institutions. Some have set up separate communities. They want to throw out the idea of integrated schools and go back to all black schools, this time with complete black control. In France you had the opportunity to start afresh, as it were. With blacks only. Did you?"

"No. I found that in Paris people of different color were interrelating with apparent ease. My office colleagues were white and nonwhite. The same thing was true of other people I met. Skin color seemed to have no special merit. Intelligence. Charm. Imagination. Humor. Money. These were concerns which influenced social intercourse. Admittedly I entered France expecting problems because of my color, but I experienced few or none of those problems. There was no longer any need to seek the company of other blacks exclusively. No pressure."

"Would you say that is the experience of all blacks in France?"

"Why should I? And how could I? Perhaps there are blacks in France who would totally disagree with me. I don't know. I've not met them. Here's a refreshing thing. On meeting blacks in Paris, it was not inevitable that we talk 'race.' We might discuss art, or money or the politics of the time. Or women. Mostly women. Occasionally race, but not inevitably race. Does that tell you any-thing?"

The train came to a shuddering stop, interrupting our con-versation. From the comments of those commuters nearest the doorways, it seemed that we were a few hundred yards short of the 125th Street station. Passengers gathered their possessions and braced themselves for an equally shuddering start. Five minutes, ten minutes, twenty minutes of grumblings and speculation, then a sudden exodus of the more impatient ones onto the tracks. We remained seated in the now more than half-empty compartment. My neighbor commenting on the irrational impatience of people, on the foolhardiness of walking beside electrified rails, on the futil-ity of so dangerously seeking to save a few minutes which would be casually wasted later over coffee or a cigarette, etc., etc. Then back to us.

"And after those four years?"

"I went on to another job."

"In Paris?"

"Yes."

Remembering those occasions while with the Veterans, meeting with senior UNESCO personnel at the international conferences in Paris and other European cities. Talking with them about educa-tion and welfare. More often about education. Drawn slowly but, it would seem, inevitably back into the wider concerns of educational theory, method and application. Those were good times. Feeling completely at ease with men with whom I shared a particular inter-est. Flattered by their occasional references to my authorship of certain remembered essays and my book. Eventually accepting the job with UNESCO in Paris. Everything moving comfortably for me. The native Guyanese with the British-passport resident in France.

Thinking about that passport and the irony of it. Treated as British when traveling in continental Europe or in Asia or in Africa. The passport was enough. Amused at the security it not only offered but guaranteed me. Outside of England. Like a protective talisman.

" . . . Valid for all parts of the Commonwealth and for all foreign countries . . . "

Taking it all in my stride. To Spain and to Italy and to Portugal. And later on making a trip to Australia and New Zealand for a UNESCO-sponsored series of lectures on education. Disembarking at Melbourne Airport after a busy schedule in New Zealand, my thoughts on a hot shower, a cool bed and long hours of relaxing sleep after that tiring flight. Handing over my passport for the immigration officer's inspection. A mere formality. I thought. Watching his careful scrutiny of each page then hearing his soft-voiced, patient query.

"Your visa, Mr. Braithwaite."

"Visa?" Caught off balance.

"Yes," he replied. "I can't find your visa for entry into Australia."

"I'm afraid I don't understand. This is a British passport."

"I can see that, Mr. Braithwaite." Unperturbedly patient.

"Well, this is a Commonwealth country, isn't it? And on page four of this passport it clearly states . . . "

"I know what is stated on page four, Mr. Braithwaite." His courtesy as keen as a razor's edge.

"Well, then, what's the problem?" Me embarrassed as hell,

acutely conscious of the interested attention around me from my fellow travelers. All white. Many of them new immigrants. English. Italian. German. Dutch. Hungarian. I'd heard them on the flight. Excited, enthusiastic about coming to Australia.

"Let me put it this way. You're not European, Mr. Braithwaite."

The gentle smile, while I got the message, the ugly contemptible message. Feeling the sudden eruption of rage, but holding tight to myself under all those eyes. The years at Cambridge contributing.

"I wouldn't have thought that you were European either," I responded. Let him chew on that for a while, then let him spell it out for me, loud and clear before these new, would-be Australians.

He was beautiful, his aplomb unruffled, confronting the only black in that small crowd. A real professional, adroitly shifting position with, "May I ask the purpose of your visit to Australia, Sir?" Holding the passport open as if any eventual decision depended entirely on whether or not my reply satisfied him. Me wishing I could somehow disturb that glacial self-assurance.

"I'm here on UNESCO business. I am sure the Residential Representative is waiting for me somewhere inside." Observing the barely perceptible change in him. He left abruptly and entered a near-by office, returning almost immediately to wave me through into Australia with my unvisaed passport.

Within the country itself, the people I met were extremely courteous and kind and helpful but my own responses were inevitably tinctured by the recurrent memory of that incident at the airport. Two weeks later I visited that other piece of Australia. The offshore island of Tasmania. Green and pleasantly rural. Over a long beer with one of the local elders we talked about Tasmania's growth and development from the "good old days" to the present. In the "good old days," he told me, the settlers would organize Sunday picnics. *Blackbirding* picnics. Groups of men would take their dogs and guns into the bush to flush out and shoot "blackbirds," a term they used to describe the hapless and helpless bands of aborigines, men, women and children, who once inhabited Tasmania. Shooting them had been the popular Sunday sport for the settler men, women and children. It was always refreshing to get back to France.

"What about your writing?"

"About this time I wrote my first novel."

"The others were all autobiographies?"

"Right."

"How was it received?"

"The reviews were very flattering."

"Was it set in France?"

"No. In London."

"I'll look forward to reading it. Tell me. Would you say that the years in France changed you? Your viewpoint, your attitude? Bearing in mind your experiences in England, most of them obviously painful, how would you compare the time spent in France with your time in England?"

He was as agile as a grasshopper. Switching from one thing to another. Telling me he'd look forward to reading my novel, yet not asking its title. Now he wanted me to make this kind of comparison. To hell with that. Why should I make such a comparison for him? Anyway, they were very different experiences. In England it was a sequence of sharp contrasts. The happy years of University and the R.A.F. The bitter years of job hunting and the early flight into teaching. Then the eight or nine years of recovery, adjustment, growth, if you like. The years in France were quite different. I went there into a well-paid job, unharried by social or economic pressures. Soon after arrival there my first book was published in French to good reviews. I was accepted into the community of artists. No strain.

"Sorry, I can't make that kind of comparison for you," I replied.

"Okay. I accept that. Another thing. You visited Africa and found yourself responsive to the fact of being there. Did you feel any strong inclination to settle in Africa, to be free of the strains and stresses which you intimate are nearly inevitable for a black person in a predominantly white society? Look, I'm not asking these questions idly or attempting to pry into your personal life. This is honestly the first opportunity I've ever had for this kind of frank discussion with a black man."

"I thought you said you knew some. Business associates and others. Haven't you talked with them? Asked them your questions?"

"Not really. After you've lived here several years you'll begin to understand. I've known many black friends over the years, but never well enough for a chat like this. Always it seems as if we meet each other with our guard up. Careful to say the right thing to each other. The acceptable thing. Like playing a game according to prescribed rules, I suppose. Going through the motions without letting ourselves become too exposed. I suppose, if you broke it down, you might say that we've never risked knowing each other." That ever-ready smile, turned on and shining.

"But you refer to them as friends," I said.

"Yes. Of course. I'm sure that we'd all pass the superficial tests of friendship. Entertain each other at home. Lend or borrow money, if necessary. Put business in each other's way. All the familiar, acceptably general things. It's possible to do them for years without knowing each other. Without testing each other's real thoughts. Without establishing the contact of truth, you might say."

In spite of the smile the words sounded flat and sterile as if he were reciting an algebraic equation. Words for words' sake.

"Then why do you believe you'd get answers from me?"

"Because we've been talking this way. Frankly. Without trying to butter each other up. Anyway, as I said, I don't want to intrude, but I just thought I could ask you."

"I don't consider it an intrusion. I went to Africa as a visitor, with a job of work to do. Not as a tourist seeking comparisons, or a displaced person seeking anchorage or a dissatisfied person feeling around for a change of environment. I was content with my work, socially comfortable and artistically motivated. I had no wish to change even though being there in Africa was a wonderful experience . . . "

Remembering it. Remembering the letter I wrote to Rudi in Paris about it:

> . . . *Our African heritage extends far beyond that which*
> *most white people know anything about. It is inclusive of*
> *nobility and pride in self and generosity one to another. As*
> *I travel through Africa, one thing I've discovered is that one*
> *needn't be hungry in Africa. If anyone has, he lets you have*
> *some of it. There is always a welcome, and any claim to*
> *kinship is a claim to participation. When we as black people*
> *talk about our blackness and our African heritage, we must*
> *include all these things. Here I've discovered the respect*
> *for the elder and respect for the leader, and respect for the*
> *person who is in a position to advise and teach, and also*
> *respect for the very young, the little ones who are growing up.*

The older ones care for the little ones and the little ones care about the older ones. The little ones help the older ones and the older ones look after the little ones.

In my blackness, I must recognise and accept all this. I must see the complete identity, not a partial identity. That identity has nothing to do with the way I dress and the way I comb my hair. It has to do with the kind of spirit I have, a spirit that will accept nothing which dehumanises it or debases it. When you're in Africa, you see the man close to the African soil. A proud man. I saw Guinea soon after it had insisted on its independence. I saw Guinea as it was raped by the French, the buildings stripped of everything that could possibly be of use so that a house vacated by a French occupant was just a shell with anything representing utility taken out.

I saw the harbor that had been destroyed; all that remained was the skeletal residue of piers sticking up out of the water. I listened to the President of Guinea speaking to his people regularly, not saying to them, "We must hate the French for what they have done." Never one instance in which I heard this. He was saying to them, "Guinea is now ours. We must build it together. Everything that has to be done, we must do it and we must take pride in doing it." He said, "Perhaps, it is a good thing the French did what they did that we might be reminded freedom never comes cheaply."

Sometimes when I reflect on him, I think to myself, "An African could stand on the soil of Africa and speak of freedom." When I'm in Europe, to what degree can I speak of freedom? Of course, I can go to bed at night without expecting that I will be removed and sold into slavery once again.

But this is not the whole of freedom. When the African speaks of freedom, he doesn't have to qualify it. When Sékou Toure talked to his people and said, "We once again possess our homeland and it is ours to build and to shape as we wish. We can either fail ourselves and our inheritors or we can establish the pattern for success," he was saying this without thinking, "This is all right but we might be limited, there is a hotel over there that might not accommodate us, there is a part of Conakry where we might not live," no such qualifications. When I think of freedom, because I am not an immediate son of Africa the whole thing becomes quite different, and I find that my freedom is curtailed in spite of myself . . .

"So you wouldn't wish to live in Africa? To settle there?"
"I couldn't answer that. I really don't know."

Reflecting, inside myself, that Africa is a huge continent, with a wide variety in peoples and customs and religions and social attitudes. I'd visited a small part of Africa and though the experience was exciting, I was only visiting. Naturally, some aspects of the visit were of special significance and meaning to me. In Ghana, for instance. I would be walking down a street and wherever I looked there would be black men and women walking tall, walking pridefully. Some of them, because of their position or social status or wealth, dressed in the glorious Kinte cloth, that beautiful hand-woven, one-piece, local robe of purple, gold and blue colors.

Ingeniously wrapped around the body, with one end thrown over the left shoulder the way ancient Romans wore the toga, the right arm uncovered; this dress seemed to dictate the regality with which they moved. Looking at these men and women I felt stirred inside myself, happy to be an extension of them.

This was for me exciting because, so recently a welfare officer in England, my extensions had been invariably humiliating when I saw other black people being abused or debased. In Ghana I felt ennobled by being part of the prevailing nobility or sense of nobility shared by everyone, prince or peasant. Going into the open-air market and moving among the traders. I felt there was something special about them as if they knew that Africa was royal earth and each of them a prince or a princess. Even I, a stranger, was allowed to share; nobody questioned my right to it. Without asking anyone's leave, I, too, could wear the mantle of nobility and move around as just me, a human being full in my skin and happy that the skin was black because blackness was beauty, blackness was nobility, blackness was grace, blackness was honor, blackness was pride, blackness was all those things for which I had been hungering so long. Blackness was personal industry and application, and a determination to independence. I could have my fill of it all, without ostentation, without noise, without posturings. Just help myself.

It was an extraordinary experience, the kind of experience that once it touches you, never leaves you. Since then it doesn't matter what the circumstances which have attempted to humiliate me, I can reflect on those moments, and walk with a sense of grace. I can walk with a sense of pride.

*　　*　　*

"Did you have a chance to get back home—to British Guiana in the course of this job?" he asked, intruding on my musings.

"No, not in the course of the job. I went back to Guyana very much later, on invitation from the government. On the eve of its independence."

"I was just wondering what you thought of it, coming back to it, as opposed to having grown up there."

"It was a very special experience. One of these days I'll discover the right words for expressing it."

I couldn't discuss it with him. He didn't really care. Even now the full import of that return was only gradually revealing itself to me. In retrospect. I'd left British Guiana, the colony, as a boy. I returned to Guyana on the eve of its becoming an independent entity and perhaps I had imagined that this would mean returning to a Guyana that would be very much like a Ghana. Perhaps I had not realized that although Ghana, too, had been colonized, the Ghanaians were on their native earth. They bore the pressures of the colonizer but all the time they bore it on their native earth. They were in touch with their continuous past and their sense of dignity had never been really disturbed. No matter what happened to them they were in touch with their earth; they had not been removed from it. Whereas in Guyana we were the offspring of the enslaved. I prefer to use the term enslaved than to use the term slave, which seems to be such a final term as if to be a slave is to be encompassed forevermore. But when one uses the term enslaved one is considering a transient situation out of which one is determined to free oneself. Returning to Guyana I discovered that of course the British were leaving, but the conditioning would remain, perhaps for a long time.

"Had the English elected to leave?"

"The colonizer never elects to leave unless the colony has been bled white and is no longer advantageously exploitable. They left Guyana only after a bitter struggle."

"I seem to recall that there was something of a civil war. Blacks against Indians. How come you never felt you should go there and fight or help—was there some kind of guerrilla movement there?"

I didn't answer that. Inadvertently he'd touched on a very sensitive spot. Oh, yes, I'd often thought of going back to join in the struggle. But it had stopped there. I lived in Europe and had my own private little battles and those battles bore out the old adage that the piece is much larger than the whole. I was struggling to live, to find myself, to overcome a situation which at one time had threatened to destroy me. Of course I was interested in the fortunes of Guyana and I sought to learn everything I could about events there. I wanted Guyana to emerge free from British control and domination; still, at no time did I feel, at no time did I imagine, that my returning to Guyana would in any way affect the general situation. Perhaps I was extremely selfish in this respect. But there it is. At the time of the struggle I did not elect to return. The truth is, I could not afford to return. Simple matter of money, or lack of it.

Reflecting that I'd not been completely out of touch. I'd met the leaders in London, in those far off days when Cheddi Jagan and Forbes Burnham were together in the struggle against the British. I met them whenever they came up to push the case for independence with the members of a resistant British Government. I'd tried to entertain them as I was able, to let them appreciate my identity with their joint struggle.

One disturbing thing on visiting Guyana again was the realiza-

tion that there was no inclination to unity now that we had rid ourselves of the oppressor. But even more than that, although he was
going, one saw plenty of evidence that we hungered for his presence. We hungered for the things that were identified with him. We
hungered for the titles that he occasionally conferred upon us—the
knighthoods and the orders. We hungered for them and we fought
and schemed for them. Perhaps because I had lived so close to those
things in Britain itself and had seen other *black knights* from other
places humiliated in the streets of London during the Notting Hill
riots and during the Birmingham riots and the Nottingham riots, I
realized that as far as the Englishman is concerned, the titled black
man is a joke. He's an anachronism—he doesn't really belong.

In Ghana men wore their regality in their skins and in their
hearts. Following their struggle for political independence they'd
revived old titles, reinstituted old social forms as part of the total
re-establishment of themselves and their nobility. The Ghanaian
had all this. And something else. He had his own language.

It's an important thing, language, because through it African
can talk to African and be sure of understanding. They can also
use the language of the stranger in order to satisfy certain circumstances which relate more to the stranger than to themselves. Yet
their own language is there, together with a variety of tribal customs which reinforce their sense of belonging and of being. Some
of these customs are steeped in ancient belief and religion, but
each one is part of the enduring ties that bind African to African,
irrespective of social and economic levels. I found it extraordinary that while in Ghana I would talk with men who had been
educated in Europe, men of substance and standing in the community, men who were considered eminent even by the stranger,
the white stranger, who is inclined to think nothing black could

really be eminent, and discover that some of these men, when ill, would seek out what is called the witch doctor in preference to the European doctor or the European-trained doctor of contemporary medicine. The problem was not with them but with me, for failing to understand the many-faceted cement which bound African to African and Africans to Africa.

They could fight with one another, they could kill one another, but they would still remain linked by a common destiny. Part of this destiny was involved with the food they ate, the clothes they wore, the language they spoke, the spirits of the living past in which they believed. In the United States it is quite different. In Europe it is different. In Guyana it is different. We have been conditioned to dependence. We have no language of our own. We were stripped of everything we possessed. More than that, we were stripped in a way which rendered us spiritually naked. We were made to see ourselves as unworthy, so it is not surprising that decades of conditioning would have produced inside of us a belief in our own inequality and insufficiency. Now we have the hard work of re-educating ourselves to an appreciation of our own worth, or our humanity, our dignity and our strength. Attaining political independence was only a beginning. The acid test of our pride in ourselves lay in our ability to make that independence work.

I can remember the first time I visited Ghana. I had a reservation at a hotel on the edge of the airport. One of the porters collected my bags in a hand truck to take them over to the hotel. He looked at the baggage tags and said to me, "You visiting Ghana?" I said, "Yes, I am a visitor." He asked me where I came from and I told him. Then he asked, "Why are you here? What are you doing here?" I said, "I've come to take a look at Ghana and find out a little about it because I do a little writing and I want to write about Ghana." He immediately stopped the truck, struck a pose and said, "If you want to know about Ghana, ask me. I am Ghana." I thought this the most extraordinary observation I had heard. He was a porter. He didn't say to me, "I am Ghanaian. Ask me about Ghana." He said, "I am Ghana." I've never forgotten that.

Here I am living in a country where no black man says to me, "I am America." Many black men say to me, "I am not American" because they feel no sense of identity with the earth that is America. However, the time must come when they will have to feel the same way about America as that Ghanaian felt about Ghana. They must feel that their blood is involved with the soil, their life past, present and future involved with the soil, and involved with it irrevocably. There is nothing that anyone can do which could excoriate their contribution from the solid state of America. And therefore if they dismiss this as unimportant, then it means that they're more rootless than they ever imagined they could be. Their dignity and their nobility must relate to them as men and as Americans.

"Tell me about your homeland, Guyana. You say you were invited to visit by the government. When was that?"

"In 1963."

"Were you offered a job with the government?"

"No."

Actually, some possibilities were discussed with me but I expressed unwillingness to accept any of them for reasons which seemed sufficiently valid to me. In the wake of the bloody interracial strife which preceded independence, Guyana became racially and politically polarized. Accepting an appointment inside Guyana presupposed identification with and membership in the ruling political party, the predominantly Negro P.N.C. (People's National Congress). This would immediately have alienated me from any meaningful contact with non-Negro Guyanese, particularly those of Indian origin. Additionally, all who had actively supported the P.N.C. and its leaders' successful bid for power understandably expected to be rewarded by political or other office. My nonparticipation in those troublous times would have been sufficient ground for their opposition to my appointment. Quite naturally, my presence in Guyana caused considerable speculation. Some of the more militant and vocal P.N.C. activists considered the foreign-based native sons expatriates who had enjoyed the good life abroad, while the faithful suffered and triumphed, and now were returning to appropriate to themselves the fruits of that triumph. I think I was enough of a political realist to appreciate their point of view. I returned to my job in Paris.

"Were you in any way tempted to resettle yourself in Guyana, as an established writer in a newly independent country? Your own country? Perhaps your very presence there would have been of considerable social significance. In any society, new or otherwise, an artistic nucleus sometimes provides the thrust towards social and political reform. Wouldn't you agree?"

Christ, the way the words poured out of him! Mention a situation and he had the answer, packaged and ready. All we needed now was a tidy little jingle to go with it. He was just using words.

What did he know about living away from one's roots because of the force of circumstances, the need to eat?

He was asking a whole spate of questions which I'd often asked myself, without giving myself any definitive answers. As a native son, I was happy to be at home, to see faces and hear voices of childhood friends; to enjoy the revival of childhood memories. I had left British Guiana an inexperienced youth full of ambition and energy. The years between had provided harsh lessons in personal survival. The idea of resettling myself in Guyana did occur to me. But as what? As a writer? I had lived all the intervening years away from Guyana. Such abilities and talents as I possessed had been nurtured or prodded into activity in conditions and circumstances very different and far removed from the Guyana scene.

I write as I am stimulated and I am stimulated as I am involved. Very soon during the visit it seemed very doubtful that I could become involved in the essential fabric of Guyanese life without declaring some political identity. No political party commended itself to me. Furthermore, I was not a full-time writer, dependent only on my literary earnings. I had a job which paid me well and which I enjoyed. I argued the matter with myself, and the argument favored returning to Europe.

"No." I told him.

"Was that your last visit to Guyana?"

"No. In 1964 I received another invitation, this time to participate in the Independence celebrations."

For me the most impressive moment of those celebrations was at a simple ceremony when the British flag was run down the flagpole for the last time, and Guyana's own national colors were unfurled to flutter in the evening breeze. For me that was a particular moment of fulfillment. I was standing close to the Duke of

Kent, the Queen's representative at the ceremony. I looked at him, resplendent in his heavy official accouterments, flushed and damp from the oppressive heat, yet coolly impassive, as if quite unaffected by so piffling an exercise.

"And still you had no wish to remain there?"

"Oh, I often wished, but inevitably the realities of living would intervene and disperse the wishes. I was grateful and happy to have been witness to so special an occasion. After all, it would happen only once in a lifetime."

"But you didn't stay?" Persistent as hell.

"No. I returned to my work in France."

Before leaving I had had a meeting with the prime minister at which he expressed the hope that native sons and daughters living abroad would feel encouraged to return home to participate in the urgent responsibilities attendant on political independence. I was invited to express my view and told him about my own reservations. His supporters would expect to benefit from his and his party's success and would be embittered by, and opposed to, the appointment of those whom they were labeling "Guyanese expatriates." I would be willing to serve Guyana if I could do so away from the mill-stream of parochial politics and in an area consonant with my experiences and ability.

"So that was the end of that."

"Yes." Thinking of leaving it there, then as suddenly deciding to give him another bit of a shock. "You may remember that early in 1965, Sir Winston Churchill died. Quite unexpectedly I received a telegram requesting me to meet Guyana's prime minister in London where he would be attending the funeral. At that meeting I was invited to join Guyana's fledgling diplomatic corps, as her ambassador to the United Nations."

"Good Lord! Just like that?"

"Just like that."

"You had no inkling it was coming?"

"None!"

"Fantastic. And you accepted."

"Yes."

"But that would be a political appointment, would it not? So you would have to, shall we say, toe the party line?"

"It was a political appointment, but there was no suggestion that I become a party member."

"Would you have refused?"

"Yes. I had already publicly stated my position on party membership. The invitation to join the diplomatic corps was made with the full knowledge of that position."

"But as an ambassador you'd have to carry out the party's dictate . . ."

"As ambassador I would carry out my government's dictate and I could tell myself that the government's decisions to some degree included opposition opinion. Perhaps it was a naïve way of accommodating a political reality, but there it is."

"So you became an ambassador. You know, you amaze me. Who would expect to find an ambassador riding in this compartment on this train? I'd bet that not another person on this train knows there's an ambassador among the passengers."

"Well, it doesn't make the train move any faster or at all, does it? Do you think that telling the driver might help?"

Laughter from him. Pleasant, relaxed. Around us the heavy quiet of impatient waiting. No rustle of newspapers. No conversation. An occasional pointedly noisy sigh accompanying a change of position but lost on those already far retracted within themselves and their private concerns. A bald man passed our seat in slow progress along the aisle to the door but made no attempt to look outside. Retracing his steps he seemed to be examining each face, his own fixed in a hopeful smile, the mouth half-opened, ready for the conversational exchange. Nothing. Perhaps no face offered the slightest encouragement to the first overture. His eyes held mine briefly as he approached. He passed us, his footsteps soon as indistinct as the sounds of traffic outside, far away.

"How long do you think we're likely to be stuck here?" I asked my neighbor.

"God only knows. Depends on what's the trouble up ahead. I was once caught like this for nearly two hours. Lucky we're not in the tunnel. I've had these trains up to here." He made a quick flat-handed gesture towards his throat. "But what can you do? Drive into the city? Then what? Where do you park? Anyway, after eight hours of the rat race, who wants to drive sixty miles?"

A sharp, prolonged whistle sounded somewhere outside. I braced myself for the pull of the train. Gradually my muscles relaxed themselves as nothing happened, even though the whistle echoed and re-echoed distantly in my mind.

I thought of us, my neighbor and me, trapped in this interlude. How would it have been if he'd been black? Easier? Friendlier? At any rate we'd have had a common point of departure. But then what? Moving inward to compare our common hostility to our common enemy? Maybe there's some satisfaction in the fellowship of experiences shared and understood. But is such satisfaction conducive to strength? Or growth? Or development?

During the bitter years in England there'd been many occasions for "hate sessions." Meeting another black encouraged the ready recital of woes. After all, the common enemy was insistently vocal in his demands for our rejection. "Keep Britain White. Ban the

Blacks." And yet, what did any "hate session" do for me or for any of us? Okay, so momentarily the internal pressure was eased. Or was it? Didn't the psychologists say that the occasional moan was a necessary safety valve? Did I ever feel relieved? Did I ever emerge from a "hate session" enthusiastic enough to occupy myself in activities conducive to improvement? Never. Now, just supposing this neighbor was black, what would we be talking about?

Here this one was doing the questioning and I was supplying the answers. Why not the other way around? Hell, there was nothing I really wanted to know about him. He was just another person, another human being. That was enough for me. I accepted the fact of his humanity, so nothing about him was likely to amaze or shock me. At least I didn't think it would. On the other hand I was sure he found me somewhat, well, amazing. He said so. Was it merely because I'd done some things immediately outside the familiar ambit of his experiences? Or was it that my being black provided a special glaze to the things I did, rendering them larger in consequence? Would a black brother have questioned me this way, and, if he did would I have been willing to answer? Would I have questioned his motives or his sincerity, or would his blackness have been enough . . . ?

"Where did you live?"

"I beg your pardon." Thinking I'd missed some of it.

"When you became ambassador to the UN did you live in New York? I know of several diplomats who live in the suburbs and commute to the city."

"I lived in New York, a few blocks from the UN."

"Were you comfortable in New York?"

Suddenly the feeling of irritation with him, just when I was flattering us on our easy association. Christ, this one here beside me was not seeing me as a man, like himself. To him I was not a sensitive, intelligent human being into whose company accidental circumstance had led him. To this bastard I was a phenomenon, a freak, possessed of the power of speech like some bloody myna bird. The nature of his questions betrayed him, in spite of the friendly pose and the ready smile. Thinking this I turned myself around to watch him. To really watch in case it might be possible to discover him behind his questions. His bloody stupid questions.

"I'm thinking of the comparisons someone like you inevitably would make between the conditions you experienced in Europe and those you've met here in the U.S." He went on. "From time to time I've read and heard complaints by black diplomats about one thing or another."

"I suppose I was as comfortable as it is possible for a black person to be in the United States," I replied. I had no intention of parading any complaints for his inspection. Without warning, the easy camaraderie had evaporated. He rearranged himself to face me, a little grimly I thought, as if readying himself for a special effort. I wondered what was coming.

"On a personal level, considering the privileges an ambassador enjoys, were you in any way inhibited by your blackness?"

Asking it then seeming to retreat from the words like someone who throws a stone, then scoots into hiding. The irritation grew, ballooned into anger. I fought it, keeping my mouth firmly shut until I could control it. Behind the display of flattery and friendliness, this son-of-a-bitch had neither seen nor heard me. All this time, after all the talk, all the shitty questions, he'd not got one inch beyond my blackness. Christ! After all these long years, nothing had changed. Nothing. Didn't the stupid bastard understand that I and my skin are one? Or did he suppose that my skin is stretched tight but wide around me like the skin of a dry gourd around the dislocated seeds rattling within? Maybe he thought that because of my education I'd somehow become pinky white inside my black skin, uncomfortable in it, inhibited by it and anxious to break out of it. Good God! The arrogance of the man! Should I bother to answer him? Hell, why not? Why let his stupidity force me to retreat into silence?

"My skin in no way inhibits me. I've had half a century of living in it. I'm accustomed to it. I'm happy in it. I am it. It is me. I know who I am and how I look, so I am free to concentrate on what I can achieve. Do you understand what I'm saying?" Keeping my eyes fixed on him, but somewhat disconcerted by the glasses which shielded his eyes behind indistinct reflections of the dirty window and the flitting scene beyond. He shifted his face away from my gaze. The anger was large in me but I felt strong controlling it. Why should I let this person have the satisfaction of knowing he could goad me to anger. So easily.

"Thank you," he said, adding, "you know, it's difficult for someone like me to ask questions of a black person without somehow sounding rude or feeling that I'm invading areas of privacy. Frankly, I've never before had an opportunity for this kind of, well, frank conversation."

I laughed without meaning to, without feeling the pleasure of laughter, taking a perverse delight in the sudden surprise on his face.

"You call this a frank conversation?" I asked, the anger threatening to overspill. "You've not been talking to me. You've been talking to my blackness. A little while ago you mentioned your black friends. If they are really your friends you should have had plenty of opportunity for talking to them, for *frank conversations* with

145

them. But I suspect you were so hung up on *their* blackness you had no time to see the men, let alone talk to them. Your confusion arises from your inability to see us. Them and me. And even that bothers you, so you try to approach it through a web of piddling excuses and apologies. Well, let me tell you a little about me, the real me, even though I doubt it will make any significant dent in your attitude. My blackness is only part of me. A small part. Perhaps the least important part. There's all the rest. My spirit, my intellect, my imagination, my strength, my nobility, my humanity. All neatly and beautifully packaged in this skin. All you see, all you dare see is the blackness and you're contemptuous of it. I see the contempt in your eyes. I hear it in your voice. Perhaps you dare not look beyond my blackness lest you see the rest of me, size, shape, weight and spirit occupying as much as or more space than you do. That would force you to acknowledge my humanity, wouldn't it? So you concentrate on what is least about me, my blackness. Okay, be my guest."

Hell, I'd not intended to blow off like that, but it came out. Cool and quiet it came out, and I didn't care one tiny damn how it sounded to him. While I spoke he'd made no movement, no sound. The only indication that he'd heard me was the irregular pattern of red spreading up from his collar.

"What about you? Do you look at us, at me?" His voice was tight.

I liked that. Yes, that was so much better than the aloof, patrician pose.

"You bet I do. Happily, more of us are looking at you. At long last we are seeing you as merely human, and not the devils we had imagined you to be. The more we appreciate your ordinary humanity, the more we'll realize that we can be as evil as you are, as ambitious as you are, as creative as you are or as dumb as you are. We can be all the things you boast of being. When we look at you and can see you as ordinary human, we'll see you as a man, not THE MAN. I look at you now and see your eyes avoiding me. Do you know, I look at you, speculating about what I see, but neither hating nor despising nor contemptuous of what I see, and therefore I am not troubled by looking. I feel free to look, even as I remember that you are not accustomed to my looking at you, and that might be the reason why you look away. I remember that only yesterday in your history and mine, the black man would be basely brutalized for looking the white man in the eye and castrated or lynched if caught looking at the white woman."

He raised a hand as if to silence me, but hesitantly, saying, "Why do you insist on making this a personal thing? Can't we have a quiet, friendly discussion without attacking each other?" tincturing it with his boyish smile.

"That's exactly what we're having, isn't it? A quiet, friendly discussion. But it is also very personal. How can I talk with you about me, and the others who are an extension of me, without being personal? You ask me personal questions, so you should be willing to have personal answers."

"Okay. Okay. But we needn't be offensive to each other, need we?"

I looked at him, amused at his irritation.

"That's one tough lesson you'll need to learn, my friend," I replied. "When you finally get around to respecting me you'll not be offended by my frank responses. Perhaps your black associates have always been concerned to avoid offending you. My only concern is to avoid discourtesy, to you or to anyone else. But I'm not worried if my honest, courteous responses offend you."

"Okay. I take your point. But isn't this very discussion we're having valid proof that a white person can see beyond the black skin and recognize the man?"

"All that this discussion demonstrates is that we are talking. You and I. That's all. It proves nothing. Here we are, thrown together by one of those accidents of fortune, and we talk. That is all it is."

"I'm sorry you take so negative a view."

"Not negative. Realistic."

After all, he and his predecessors had had at least a couple of centuries of exposure to me. Plenty of time in which to recognize and acknowledge me, if they'd so wished. Yes. There was a time when I really believed that I was shrouded in an invisibility which permitted them to live and move, unconscious of my presence. I have now completely abandoned that belief. They have always seen me. More than that, they have always been acutely aware of me, but have not dared look closely at me lest they discover my humanity, lest they discover my nobility, or perhaps for fear that they might discover my pride and the warnings implicit in the acknowledgement of my pride. It was comfortable for them to stop at my blackness.

"Don't you think you could be wrong in assuming that your blackness is all that's seen and recognized by us? Why should you be the only ones capable of insights beyond the superficial skin fabric. Much of what you say suggests the same double standard attitude of which you accuse us."

"Is that what you'd like to believe?" I asked.

"It's what seems to be the case. Anyway, what I'd begun to ask is how you, a black ambassador, relate to the American community. Among the people. After all, ambassadors can't confine all their time and interests to the United Nations."

Again he was doing his trick of combining questions and statement while sneakily slipping away from the discussion which obviously disturbed him. So why the hell should I follow his leap-frogging from idea to idea? How I spent my time privately was my own business. Perhaps he entertained the familiar view of ambassadors, dinner-jacketed at operas, theatres and parties, kissing the perfumed fingers of elegant women, hobnobbing with the wealthy and titled. Champagne and caviar. Okay, he was welcome to his imaginings. But why did he assume that black ambassadors would be different, lead different lives?

"Have you ever met an ambassador? Besides me?"

"Well, not socially. My organization once did some promotional work for one of the Trade Missions. From Spain. The ambassador gave a cocktail party . . . "

"Then, if you've seen one, you've seen them all," I interrupted him. I knew that nothing I could say would change his view that blacks would *naturally* behave differently from whites, at any social or economic level. *Blacks* were not people. They were a disturbing phenomenon within the social scene, forcing attention on themselves. First black is named to City's Board. Mayor appoints first black to . . . President names first black . . . First black is appointed to run city's prisons. Always attention is focused on the blackness. Not on ability or qualification. Blackness. What did this one here suppose a black ambassador did? Publicly they easily proved themselves capable at the highest levels of office. United Nations Under-Secretary-General. President of the General Assembly. President of the Security Council. Maybe he discounted all that. So why should their private lives suggest any peculiar patterns or dimensions?

I, personally, had had perhaps more opportunities than most for public contact. Many Americans had read my books. Particularly the first one. When my appointment to the United Nations was announced I received hundreds of congratulatory messages, especially from the teaching fraternity and students of colleges and high schools. I was invited to visit and address colleges and schools in many states and in turn invited them to visit the Guyanan Mission in New York to observe at firsthand something of its functioning.

They came. Groups of them. Black and white. Separately and together. The white ones took the visit easily in stride, expecting and accepting that a "black" country would have a black ambassador, black diplomatic staff, black consular and clerical staff. Even the presence of an occasional white face did not disturb them. They knew that opportunities for similar positions could be available to them in their own diplomatic service, provided they chose diplomacy as a career and were willing to live through the long processes of progressive promotion. They questioned me about my country, its peoples, its political philosophies, its resources and products, its historical and contemporary directions. Probing questions, indicative of careful rehearsal and research.

The black ones were more deeply affected and impressed by the fact of a black ambassador and staff, so like themselves but *different*. Alien. They could accept the idea of a black foreign diplomat. The rare instances of a black American diplomat were unknown to them and their questions reflected their disbelief that any of them could ever hope to achieve such high office. My attempts at assurance to the contrary were quickly brushed aside. "They'd never let us be ambassadors," one of them told me. I understood that by "they" he meant "whites."

Those black students were from so-called integrated schools, in the same classrooms with their white peers, sharing the same teachers and facilities, but not the same hopes and aspirations. The barrier against entry into certain pursuits was too real. They were not devoid of ambition or its aggressive drives, but had no wish to waste those drives futilely battering at doors they believed would remain closed. From their questions and comments I learned that they were bursting with ambition and energy. They were unafraid of hurdles in the path of an attainable goal. The studious grind. The hard work. Continuous practice. All that was partial to the goal itself. Yes, hurdles were familiar. They could be dealt with. Barriers were different. They were deliberately and intentionally designed to render the goal unattainable. Or nearly so.

"Did you get around in the community?" this neighbor was asking. "Among the people? The ordinary people?"

"All people are ordinary," I answered.

"Did you have any contact with them in their everyday surrounding?" he persisted, ignoring my barbed reply.

"Certainly. Particularly young people. Students."

"In their schools?"

"Sometimes. At other times in my office."

"I'm sure they must have been excited to meet the author of *To Sir, With Love*. Especially those who saw the movie."

"They were. But we talked about other things."

"I hope you didn't tell the black ones that their blackness forever doomed them to nothingness in the American society." Saying it with that now familiar smile, but really not meaning the smile. Something in his voice gave him away. I felt relaxed and controlled.

"No, I told them of the times and experiences which together prepared me for the post. They were particularly interested in my early years in Guyana, the schooldays of my childhood. Blacks and whites in the same elementary school, competing in the same examinations at eight years of age for entry to the secondary schools. And the other examinations. Always the examinations."

Remembering my return to Guyana in 1964 and visiting the old school house which had changed so little in the intervening years. One of my former teachers, Miss Imla Friday, still alive and active. The honor roll on the wall with the names of the high achievers, mine among them. The pride which threatened to burst me the day my name was added to the list, the same pride reflected in my mother's face.

"Integrated schools, I take it."

"What else? The single imperative was learning. The system required it. The teachers demanded it. Parents encouraged it." Think of it now, I believe those black American students were surprised to hear me say that their own so-called "ghetto" schools were considerably better equipped than those in which I had my early education. Irrespective of how poor they were, Guyanese parents bore the whole cost of every notebook, textbook, pen, pencil and anything else their children needed, so the pressure to learn, to compete successfully, was constant.

"You think it's different here?"

"For blacks it is. In Guyana we all had access to the highest levels of education available within the country, and for those who could afford it, the highest levels available outside our country, provided we could meet the academic requirements for entrance. By comparison with your standards our schools were primitive. We were short of plant and equipment and books. But we were spurred on by ambition, competition and achievement. Parents, children and teachers believed that learning was the open sesame to the good life; the harder the student worked the greater his rewards."

"That has always been and still is true for us."

"Is it? For something to be true people must believe in it, and to believe they must see it happen among themselves. During my childhood in Guyana there were the many living examples of success for me to emulate. The lawyers, doctors and others, mainly trained in England and returned to pursue successful careers. Inevitably for me and other youngsters, our sights were set on these same English universities, but that was only because we had no similar institutions at home to foreshorten the view. What mattered is that we believed in ambition and our ability to achieve. Few young American blacks share that belief. As I see it the long decades of proscriptions brutally enforced have marked black youngsters in their most private place—their ambition. Very few are prepared to embark on the unfamiliar."

"But they're in school, so they have the opportunity to learn and develop. If they fail to achieve, the fault is with themselves and their teachers, I would suppose." Cool again. Controlled again. Comfortably ready to dismiss the whole thing with those few words. Unwittingly pushing me further and further towards the edge of anger. Why the hell was I bothering to discuss it with him?

"Let's not assume that schools by themselves are all-important," I said. "They are merely complementary to the multitude of other teaching agents which surround us. Their function should be to help and encourage our understanding of the things we see and hear, and to take that understanding further and deeper. Your children, the white ones, see and hear, and believe in their entitlement to success. Their schools re-enforce, develop and channel that belief into productive effort. Do you agree with that?" Patient as hell with him.

"I'm listening. Go ahead with the point you're making."

"Your children are taught that they represent the American majority, the whites, and that everything within your social and economic system is designed to ensure the comfort and security of that majority. They are the heirs to the land of the free. They are the "all" for whom the Constitution promises freedom and justice. Are you with me?"

No answer.

"Now let's look at the others. Particularly the descendants of the slaves. The noninheritors. The nontitlists. They are reminded daily that they are "the minority," allowed by your grace and favor to have the jobs you do not want; to live in the houses and districts you have abandoned. Their children have no entitlement. To read or hear or watch any news coverage is to be reminded that they are excluded. Busing. Integration. Desegregation. Low-income housing. Zoning laws. Burning crosses against a darkening sky. You name it. Through television these issues are piped right into their homes, fed into them with each mouthful of food, each lungful of air. For them, ambition cannot be sufficient in itself. It needs to be supported by the belief in opportunity, and demonstrated within their familiar environment. Would you agree?"

"Are you suggesting that there are no ambitious blacks? That no black children are stirred by the urge to achieve? Sorry, I don't buy that. Do you know anything about our national games? Baseball? Football? Basketball? They're dominated by blacks who are paid fabulous sums. Wouldn't you call them ambitious?"

"Not particularly. Blacks are capable of much more than crude physical effort. Or even controlled, trained physical effort. There are far more nonathletic people in the world than there are athletes. Black or white. So what about the black youngster who is not interested enough or coordinated enough to become an athletic star? What of his intellect? Why do you insist on seeing us only in terms of muscles? I'm not impressed by the ballplayers who become rich. They become rich only because their special prowess makes the whites who employ them even richer. Do you realize that, were the outlets available, many blacks who have become ballplayers might have set their sights and interests and imagination to work on other areas of attainment? The law? Medicine? Engineering? Architecture?"

"So you're saying that the schools are a waste of time, for blacks?"

"No." Keeping the anger down. Cooling it. "I'm saying no such thing. I'm telling you that for white children the school complements the out-of-school life. For blacks there's very little in the schools and even less in their out-of-school life which fosters development and ambition. Most of it is spent in a state of frustration with everything around them, including home and parents. So what's there for the schools to complement? Frustration? Apathy? Rage? Is that a condition conducive to ambition?"

"I suspect you're deliberately bending certain things to suit your argument. I see many instances of ambitious blacks making it to the top. Not athletes nor entertainers. Professionals in other fields. Congressmen and women. Employees in state and federal positions. Aren't they ambitious?"

"Why certainly. But each case is another example of survival in grim spite of prevailing pressures to the contrary. Talk with any of them and you'll soon discover that each had to create his own area of belief in himself without recourse to the community around him. Whites succeed because of opportunities to success. A few blacks make it in spite of the near absence of opportunity. See the difference?"

"I'm afraid it's you who have failed to see the difference." His face still holding the muscular framework of a smile, but the voice touched with sarcasm. "There's no moratorium on ambition. Not in this country. I'm talking to you about people I know who get up and make an effort for themselves. They don't sit around bemoaning their fate and blaming others. They move. They reach. They succeed. If they're black you casually dismiss it as a tactic of survival. Well. What about the others? The ones who do so little to help themselves? Don't they also need to survive? I don't know anything about your country or Africa or the conditions in Europe. But I know something about my own country. There's always room for the man who's determined to improve himself."

He paused. I said nothing, waiting for him to get on with it. Once again he'd put aside the stuffy, aloof pose and was letting the things inside him flow even though the words still came out stiff and stilted. Hell, I should try to keep him that way, just off balance. Then I'd hear the real story, straight from the depths where he kept it neatly packaged and secured.

"A problem we face in this country is with those blacks who want everything to change overnight. Wave a wand and the pumpkin becomes a golden coach. Just like that. Have-nots into haves. No strain. No effort."

Looking at me for comment but getting none. Without warning the thing was in my guts again, tying them up. Something about him, his voice, something getting to me. Maybe the snide emphasis he'd put on the words when he'd said "those blacks."

"I believe in change," he continued, "I believe in social evolution. I believe in the concept of equal opportunities for all. But I also believe that those opportunities must be earned. People should earn their way, whether it be an education or a job. That would ensure that they appreciate what they have. That's the American way."

I was tempted to ask where all that was taking us, but thought I'd let him run on. Patience, the man said.

"I'm a liberal," he said, "and I hold the view that a black skin or any other skin should be no barrier to progress. But I'm against being pressured or being held to ransom."

"Who's holding you to ransom?" I'm not very patient. I wanted to know what was bugging him.

"You're an educated man," he went on, ignoring my question, "a highly qualified man. When one thing didn't work for you, you tried another. I don't suppose it was easy. Nothing important is ever easy. You say you hated the conditions. You say you even hated the people. But you worked. You earned their respect. Over here we have a different situation. People without skills or aptitudes clamoring for the better-paid jobs and professions, for the best in education and housing. Contributing nothing, but wanting everything. Making no effort to earn it. Demanding it. I'd be the first to admit that the blacks in America have had a raw deal. I can understand people wanting to change their state, improve their condition. That's fine. And they should be helped in every way. By the government. By the state. By individuals. But I think it would be wrong to hand things over to such people just because they demand them. Changes and improvements must be earned. By sweat. By imagination. By effort. That's been the experience of every immigrant group to this country. But these extremists want it handed to them, or they threaten to take it all."

Warming to it, as if it had touched something active beneath the well-groomed, controlled exterior. The rage was blossoming inside me, for out of a distant memory his words were a bitter echo. Coming out of a similar smooth pink face, under lowering English skies in an English Midlands town. Griffiths, that smooth, friendly Englishman who launched himself into the House of Commons on skids greased with similar sentiments. I wondered what far visions this one saw.

He wasn't funny, and yet I felt myself smiling. Not amused. Merely smiling. Not at what he said, or even the way he said it, but at him and me. At the realization that we had been circling each other, exploring each other, to reach this. We'd skirted the trifling hills and dales, skimmed the freshets and tributaries of conversation to reach this mainstream. Race. In recent years whenever I'd sat down in conversation for longer than a few moments with a white person, inevitably we'd arrive at a discussion of race.

His voice was quiet but intense, as if he'd long known and rehearsed each word in his mind. I shifted my position to face him as frontally as the seat would permit, needing to look at him, to see him in relation to the way he spoke. The man and the words and the nuances.

"Who are they? The extremists?" I asked.

"Those fellows with their bushy hair and wild rhetoric. You can hardly open a newspaper or switch on the television without seeing or hearing them and their threats. Why the media give them so much coverage is beyond me. Some of them even carry guns. Publicly. To show their contempt for those whose main concern is to build and create and conserve. They want to kill and destroy."

So controlled he was. All that intensity harnessed neatly into soft vowels and consonants. Laying it out about bushy hair and wild rhetoric. He meant blacks, of that I was sure. Saying it to me. Another black. Making it seem as though by being a stranger, I was different from the rest of the blacks, so he could tell me about them. All right, neighbor, let's see how different I am.

"Would you consider me an extremist?" My voice matching his in control. Again that smile on his face, bringing to it a certain wistful appeal. I wondered whether it was spontaneous or part of his cultivated client-softening repertoire.

"Don't be silly," came the smiling response. "No extremist would be sitting here holding such a conversation with me. I've heard them. They're demanders, threateners, not inclined to reason as you are."

Something about the smile was irritating the hell out of me. All he could see, all he saw were the suit and the black face; he couldn't see the pride. All he heard were the unfamiliar accent and the familiar use of a language he could claim as his. He couldn't hear the rage. The accent told him I was a stranger and different. But how the hell could he see me as different when the very code by which he lived stipulated that my blackness was my dominant characteristic, common to all those he'd been conditioned to despise. The readily recognizable perennial barrier between him and me. Not my intellect. Not my imagination. Not my physical strength. Not my integrity. My blackness. My ineradicable seal of kinship with all the brothers. I was trying to keep the thing inside me under control but feeling it running away with me. This son-of-a-bitch, what the hell did he know about me? Who the hell gave him the right to tell me what kind of black man I was? This same bastard who, only a short while ago, had made such a production of taking an empty seat beside me. Now his glance at me was somewhat nervous and again I could feel his retreat.

"You think I couldn't be an extremist because of my education? My, what you call, reasonableness? Well, I've news for you. In the final analysis none of that means a damned thing. Not to you. Not to whites. For as long as blacks are tractable and submissive, everything's fine. The moment we challenge you we become extremists. The moment we give any indication of thinking and acting to promote our dignity and humanity, we disturb you. Right?"

"I wouldn't say that. Not at all. I am not disturbed. I am never disturbed by blacks who promote themselves and uplift themselves. As a matter of fact I am associated with several organizations and institutions designed and operating to encourage exactly that sort of thing." Distant but controlled.

"Designed by whom? Operated by whom? By the brothers? No. By you. Always you in the driver's seat patronizing the hell out of us. Don't you ever see us as able to determine our own directions? Our own conduct?"

"What do you mean by brothers?"

"The great international fraternity. The wretched of the earth. Blacks. Extremists."

"I never suggested that all black persons were extremists." That edge again in his voice as if stresses and strains were adversely affecting his insistent, friendly pose.

"You don't suggest it, but you create the conditions which make it inevitable. Not merely for some. For all the brothers and sisters." Using the term brothers deliberately to needle him. "The very nature of his life makes a brother an extremist. From birth to final breath he is forced to live in extreme circumstances."

"I cannot agree with that. I know several colored persons, some of them business acquaintances, colleagues, who are not extremists. In fact, they have very little sympathy with the extremists."

"Oh, yes, I was forgetting that you have many black friends. The ones you cannot have a personal conversation with. So how can you know what they are or what they think? Weren't you sure I was not an extremist? What do you know of their real beliefs, their real feelings? Even about you? What do you know of such brothers apart from what they let you know of themselves? Business acquaintances, you say? Which brother can be one of your business acquaintances without having lived through the experience of rejection or discrimination at some point? Which one?"

"I don't think any of them would agree with you."

"Their disagreement with me is of no consequence. It's worth as much as their agreement with you. They need to survive and can readily persuade themselves that the means justify their ends. But the fact remains that to be what they are, to become what they have become, required that at some point they lived through extreme terms and circumstances."

"I'm sure I don't know what that means."

The train was maintaining a smooth, stable run. He uncrossed his legs and crossed them again, still holding that sideways position as if to emphasize his relaxation and control. Fine with me.

I went on, "Okay, I'll explain. Think of a young brother in one of your schools. Let's say one of your 'integrated' schools, because I'm discovering that integration is the big thing in your education system, the mind-boggling concept of a black child sitting and being taught beside a white child. Not learning, because that's not your affair. Merely being taught. Academically."

"Surely that's up to him," he intervened.

"Is it? Is it also up to a white child whether or not he learns? Anyway, never mind that. I'll tell you what the young brother discovers, what you make absolutely sure that he discovers. If he is ever to achieve anything or amount to anything in this success-oriented society, he must do more, much more than is required of his white peer. In every area of endeavor he must prove himself extraordinary in order to achieve the ordinary. He must be outstanding even where mediocrity is the norm for whites. Whatever he does must be done, one might say, extremely. In school, in seeking or competing for employment, in housing, in everything. Inevitably, therefore, when he is able to examine critically the pressures imposed upon him, and when he resists those pressures or shows some inclination to resist those pressures, the habit of extreme effort is continued. And you suddenly become shocked at this. You don't mind his being an extremely good athlete, an extremely capable soldier, an extremely obedient slave or servant, or an extremely demoralized welfare recipient. Why should you? That's all part of his familiar role, acceptable to you. But the moment he becomes extremely conscious politically, or extremely active politically, you become alarmed. Only then you see him as extremist."

"Aren't you deliberately attempting to oversimplify the situation?" he retorted. "There are hundreds of blacks who are politically conscious and active without being extremists. You know that as well as I do. Senators. Congressmen. Professionals. Others. No one could call them extremists. Even yourself. In spite of what you say I wouldn't call you an extremist."

"Whether you would or not is of no consequence. And the word is senator, not senators. There are those who, like myself, do not publicize their extremism. Perhaps we have learned to deal with it inside ourselves. Perhaps we have learned or are learning to control it, or channel it, or repress it or suppress it according to our interests, our priorities or our needs. But it is there just the same."

The thing was running away with me, surprising me, shocking me with its intensity. This stranger had really neither harmed me nor abused me, nor said anything insulting or defamatory. Yet, so quickly, as if too long dormant and impatient of awakening, the rage had overtaken me, holding me helpless. Side by side, the stranger and I were no longer neighbors but adversaries suddenly separated by an isolation layers of generations thick. A few moments of conversation, quite idle conversation, had produced this. Idle conversation, because I could not believe that any of it really meant anything more to him than a momentary topic about which he could try to be impressively knowledgeable.

He nervously shifted in his seat. Perhaps I had startled him, for though we had spoken in low tones, the inescapable vigor in my voice must have conveyed some hint of the internal violence with which I struggled. Yet, when he spoke his voice was still quite controlled, his attitude patient, even conciliatory.

"Do you make no distinction between people like yourself and those who demonstrate their extremism by bombing and burning buildings? Do you feel any identity with them? You've been using the term 'brothers.' Do you really feel that close to them?"

Again that question which quickly burrowed deep down into the private place where I lived. Did I really feel that close to them? How could I truthfully answer that? I wanted to feel close but differences imposed awful strains upon the similarities between us. Perhaps the problem was lodged in our background. I was not afraid of whites. I'd grown up with them, through all the activities of youth in Guyana and the later times of academic and athletic competition in England. They were favored for employment and that favor extended into many other areas. But I'd never feared them. Nor hated them until my personal progress was so obviously restricted and denied. Yet, even in my state of hatred there was no fear. My childhood in Guyana was happy and comfortable. No terror stalked the nights. No burning crosses. No bloodthirsty lynch gangs. No punitive posses. No vigilantes.

Blacks were men. Whites were men. Privileged, but yet merely men. The lines were crossed and recrossed. The occasional fair-skinned child born to a black mother, or the dark-skinned child born to the wife of English planter or police commissioner or administrator or banker. Myself too young then to understand the references to a cuckoo in the nest. England, Ireland, Scotland, France, Scandinavia, Germany. I'd lived and worked among whites, still aware of the privileges, but never afraid of them. Never personally threatened by them. Having no background of terrifying experience such as so many American blacks could relate to me. I'd traveled through Europe, caught overnight in many a tiny village or hamlet and entered with assurance through the doors of the local hostelry or inn or hotel. Whatever was available. No fear.

In the United States the blacks lived different lives, and those lives had colored their outlook and their attitude towards whites. I was born outside that outlook, but each day of living in the American community brought it closer to me, made it more acutely understandable, reduced the areas of difference into insignificance. In the eyes of the host community I was merely another black; I could not afford the luxury of isolating myself from the common cause. In this train, at this time, this one beside me would tell me I am different, merely because he was sitting beside me. Had he been fortunate enough to find himself another seat I would have remained a part of the blackness which he claimed threatened him and others like him. From the distance of another seat he would readily have accepted my identity with the brothers, the bombing, burning brothers. So, let's keep it that way.

"Distinctions? Yes. Of course there are distinctions. But there is also identity. I am identified with every other brother. In fact you identify me with every brother. My black face is enough. Yes, I feel identity with the brothers, and I don't care who they are. We are all subject to your general ostracism and contempt, aren't we?"

"So you would bomb and burn as they do?"

"As who do?"

"Any of the extremists who bomb and burn. The Black Panthers, for instance." I thought about that awhile.

"I'm wondering why you've selected the Panthers as your example of violence. However, let me say this. I identify with every black brother and sister, whoever they are, wherever they might be. This does not mean that I support whatever they do or say. But why the Panthers? I've not heard of them bombing or burning anywhere."

"They've declared themselves antipathetic to this country's laws and order, and dedicated to violence. Armed violence."

"Is that right? I must confess that perhaps you're better informed about them than I am. I have read that they announce themselves determined no longer to put up with abuse or ill treatment, and have stated their intention to defend themselves, violently if necessary. It seems to me that the operative word here is defend. Perhaps they anticipated and expected a need to defend themselves."

"Only because they deliberately brandished firearms, assumed postures and made inflammatory statements of violent intent against the police, the courts and every symbol of well-constituted authority. No well-ordered society can ignore or condone such threats."

"You amaze me. You really do. What is so special about the Panthers? The name? Well, let's try another for sound. What about the Ku Klux Klan? Surely that's a name which conjures up a record for violence the Black Panthers could never emulate. Terror by night. Bombings. Burnings. Lynchings. You name it. And its membership in some instances boasts impressive names. To date, the Panthers have not bombed or burned anywhere. If the information media are to be believed, the only victims of Panther violence are themselves Panthers. And even that remains very much in the realm of speculation."

I had cooled off somewhat. Perhaps it was all this talk about the Panthers. Or it may have been him. His general coolness. Here and there the hint of discomfort, but generally cool, controlled.

"We are both laymen in this matter," he said. "We have to depend on published opinions, observations or informed guesses for what we know of them. But the police are professionals. The record of their encounters with the Panthers speaks for itself. Same thing with the FBI. They publicly named the Panthers as a real and present threat to the American society. Do you discount all that?"

"I do not discount it. Nor do I set too great store by it. The recently published disclosures of police harassment and murder of Panthers in Chicago also speaks for itself. I do not share the popular view that the Panthers are really dangerous, except to themselves. It may be that their very name attracts violent police reaction. I don't know. I sometimes wonder whether we'd have heard so much about them if they'd not displayed their arms for public attention and their philosophy for public scrutiny."

"If they weren't black. Is that what you mean?"

"That's not what I meant, but it's an idea. Forming a group, arming it and cementing it together with some kind of philosophy is quite familiar on the American scene. You and I hear and read of such groups. Vigilantes, they're called. They're dedicated to violence, aren't they? No matter what excuses they plausibly advance. But that the brothers should emulate this kind of activity is more than you can bear, because the public declaration to defend themselves violently is new to you. The drawer of water, the hewer of wood, the second or third-class citizen, yes. That's the familiar image of the brother. You've long been accustomed to him servile, cowed, uneducated, grateful. The new image is too much for you."

"You know, you never answered a question I asked earlier. Do you condone the violence they advocate? Against the police? Even against their own membership?"

"I thought I'd answered that. I don't condone violence either by them or against them. But why all this talk about the Panthers and violence? Yours is a violent society. The gun is a far more familiar symbol than the Bible or apple pie. It is the linchpin of your continuing folklore. You live with it. In it. By it. In the course of any twenty-four hours you see a gun many times. In shop windows. On bank guards. On policemen. On children at play. Wherever you go the gun is there ahead of you."

Remembering the day not long ago when, new to the convoluted layout of the East Village, I'd got myself hopelessly lost. I spotted a policeman strolling slowly along a street and drove up to stop alongside of him. I rolled down my near-side window and called to him. As he approached the car his right hand reached down surreptitiously to free the flap of his holster. Perhaps an unconscious gesture, the result of continuous practice. Obviously with no ill intent towards me because we exchanged courtesies and I went my way well directed. But with a feeling of dread. What if I had made some gesture, innocent in itself but seeming to him threatening? Would his reflex action have been to draw and shoot, all part of a conditioned, self-preserving response? The image stayed with me.

A bright, handsome young man forced by the circumstances of his life and work to depend on the gun for his survival. Violent means in a violent society. That dependence increasing with each day's dangers. The wonder was that he yet remained courteously human. What was that Biblical bit about those who live by the sword? Yes, I'd seen the photographs of armed Panthers. What had it brought them? Young men and women, beautiful, intelligent, strong, gifted, setting themselves up as targets and inviting the licensed hunters to open season. Waste. Sheer waste. At this point in their history black Americans need all their resources, particularly their human resources. To see these resources frittered away so casually, so brutally, is deeply saddening. Each death reduces the whole. Each imprisonment reduces the whole. Cleaver. Hampton. Jackson. Seale. All the others. Men of intellect, imagination, ability. Perhaps every state of resistance demands its sacrifices, but need the sacrifices be made so blindly?

My neighbor had removed his spectacles and was watching me. Speculatively. Weighing in his mind what I had said or whatever it was he intended to say? A thought popped into my head. I asked him, "What would you say if I told you I was a Panther?"

This time the smile was forced. The facial muscles twitched obediently but the eyes took no part in the action.

"You must be kidding."

"Yes. I'm kidding." Reading him. It would require very little to convince him. Black and Panther. Panther and black. He'd have no difficulty making the transposition.

"I'm thinking of what you said a moment ago." The spectacles held up against the light for his inspection. "Does all that mean you are opposed to violence? Would you call yourself nonviolent?"

I'd never faced that question before. Not about myself. All my life I've been plagued by a temper quickly stirred into raging proportions, and all my life I've struggled to contain and control it. Well, perhaps, not all my life. During my boyhood my parents had applied the control, most often painfully. Always with the warning that my violent temper would bring me grievous trouble. Always I was punished for giving way to it. Punished, even when believing myself in the right, knowing that my anger and its violent expression were fully justified.

Ten years old and playing marbles with a neighbor's son in the backyard of his home. Lucky and winning. His irritation and hostility keeping pace with his losing streak. Continuing to play and his continuing to lose, the glossy spoils heavy in my pocket. The final game and his outburst of rage as I reached to collect my winnings. Snatching it up and cursing. "Stinking nigger." Tears of frustration rolling down his cheeks. White cheeks. Portuguese cheeks. Soon to become streaked and bloodied as I dived at him and punched him to the ground. Dragged him to the garden faucet and opened the jet stream on his face while punching him into submission. Pulled off him by his father and brothers who screamed that I was trying to drown him and murder him. Hauled home, his father doing all the talking, complaining to my mother. Myself silent because no child was allowed to contradict any grownup. Knowing that I'd be punished. For half drowning Johnny Nascimento, for getting my clothing soaked and muddied and for the words which the elder Nascimento claimed I'd used to him.

Tearfully explaining to my mother about the game and the names which Johnny, the loser, had called me. Knowing inside myself that the names had meant nothing, but the sight of him grabbing up the final glossy marble! It was mine. I'd won it. "Sticks and stones," my mother reminded me, the strap rising and falling.

"You could have killed that 'Portagee boy.'" Was there in her voice a measure of contempt? She never had any difficulty with the word Portuguese, but then, yes, then she said "Portagee." Her rage was greater than mine. In later, more mature years I've wondered why. The "Portagee boy" and I were never reconciled.

"Would you call yourself nonviolent?" He repeated the question.
    "I don't know," I said.

Answering as much for myself as for him. Maybe more for myself. Intellectually I argue with myself that violence is wasteful. Stupidly wasteful. Especially for those of us, those of us blacks, who are without strength. Strength of arms. Strength of money. Violence and strength are natural partners. Bedmates. Whenever violence is used successfully those who use it are powerful enough or influential enough or rich enough to control the aftermath of that violence. They are able to ensure that the results of violence are favorable to themselves, and they are powerful enough to be unaffected by any unfavorable results. The rich and influential can be casually, brutally violent. They can afford to be violent.

Outside Africa black people are neither numerous enough nor influential enough to benefit from violence. Intellectually I argue this with myself. Emotionally, I'm not so sure. Each of my own violent outbursts has satisfied something in me. Temporarily. The sight of Johnny Nascimento's puffed and bleeding face satisfied something in me. Sure he kept the marble, but he'd not be able to enjoy it for a very long time. After the sting of my own beating had subsided I thought with relish of what I'd done to him. Other times in other places there had been other prods to violent outburst. The white mouth always ready with the final epithet "stinking nigger." Jesus Christ! What's in a word? "Sticks and stones may break my bones but words can never hurt me," my mother often quoted to me, but the sticks and stones have never bruised any deeper than the skin. The words with their contempt have pierced skin and spirit to lodge themselves deep in the pride. Why had I reacted so violently to Nascimento? It was the very first time I'd been called "nigger." And yet I had reacted out of an immediate subliminal understanding of the contempt in the word. Sticks and Stones! Through the long empty months job hunting in England I'd felt the sticks and stones of rejection. I'd lived with them, exposing myself to them day in, day out. But the words?

That day in Stepney, 1950, and reasonably secure with my teaching job and the persistent hope of still finding a crack in the high wall around engineering technology. Still sending the applications. Waiting at the bus stop for the homeward-bound bus. Joined there by an attractive young brunette who kept a sterile distance between us. Eyes averted. Soon, in the near distance and approaching, three youths, noisy, playfully punching and jostling each other. Pausing near the girl, then surrounding her. Not touching, walking around her, appraising her legs and hair and face and dress. Outbidding each other in ribald commentary. Myself ignored. Dismissed after a casual glance. The girl pale. Terrified. No place to run. No help in sight. The youths bolder. Touching. The girl looking wildly around. At me.

"Why don't you fellows leave the young lady alone?" Prompted by no Sir Galahad notions, but disliking the bullying. The three of them on one.

"You talking to us?" One of them turned to look at me, jerking his head to clear the scraggy hair from his eyes. Moving towards me, thumbs hooked in his brass-studded belt. His companions following, deploying themselves on either side of him to confront me. Near.

"You talking to us, nigger?" Tough. So tough.

"I said why don't you leave the young lady alone?" Cold inside, the rage ready, waiting to explode. The talking one made a movement with his arm.

Those years of training in unarmed combat rushing back upon me. February, 1941, at Cranwell College and the Canadian instructor saying, "Watch their eyes. A guy plans to come at you, you see it in his eyes. When you see it, move. Don't wait for him to connect. You wait and you're dead. Move. Move. Get him first." Hearing it again in my head. Feeling the thrill in my guts. Dropping my brief case and reaching for the nearest one, my right hand jabbing stiff-fingered for his solar plexus, swinging the elbow sideways against his face as it jackknifed downward. Letting him fall. Feeling the kick high on my right thigh from another. Turning and closing with him, my hands around his head, pulling his unprotected face suddenly hard to meet my forehead. The squelchy sound of his mashed nose. His scream as I let him go. The third already in flight, his companions on the ground. The girl staring open-mouthed, voiceless. I picked up my brief case. Nothing to be done about my blood-spattered shirt front and coat. The two scrambling to their feet and away, the cursing a mumbled wake like the dull throbbing in my right thigh. The bus arrived and the girl hurried on to sit way up front, far away from me.

Am I a violent man? I had no intention of giving him any further answer. Perhaps he'd make his own judgment about me, just as he decided I was no extremist, because he could not know that everything in my life, everything in the life of a black man or woman, prods towards violence. Life is lived on the razor's edge of violence, with hope and rage the counterbalancing forces. Equilibrium depending on nothing more than a word, or a glance or a small gesture. Hating the idea of violence and vainly attempting to adjust to it. Recognizing its presence within the pressures and proscriptions. Where to live? Where to work? Where to eat? Where to play? Where to be hospitalized? Where to be buried? Where to be born? Living with the rage night and day. Eating with it. Sleeping with it. Constantly aware of its growth and power. Knowing that in the eye of my rage was the seed of my own destruction. So living with it, carefully, each step an achievement of dangerous balance. Needing so little for disaster. So very little.

My memory recreating the incident which happened a few days before Christmas, 1970, at the Audemars Piguet offices at Park Avenue in the Grand General Building. I'd gone there to collect a wristwatch which I'd handed in a month earlier for repairs. An expensive but lovely bauble, I'd bought it while serving as ambassador in Venezuela. What with diplomatic tax exemption and the special price quoted for diplomatic personnel, it seemed too good an opportunity to miss, apart from being an excellent watch. The guarantee stipulated that repairs be undertaken only by bona-fide Audemars Piguet representatives. The dial was slightly damaged and the watch also needed to be cleaned and regulated. On my earlier visit to the office I was waited on by one of their staff, a charming sister, who received the watch and advised me that within a month I'd be notified that it was ready to collect. By postcard. So there I was again.

The same sister came to serve me, accepting the postcard and my ownership slip which she used to locate the watch from among others in a cabinet. She handed it to one of her colleagues whom I guessed was the cashier; she, in turn, made an invoice of charges and tax and called to me, "Did Mr. Braithwaite send a check?"

That's all it took to nudge the dormant rage into full wakefulness. Looking at her white face I read it so clearly. She had glanced at me, black me, and decided I could not own such a watch. Too expensive for the likes of me. I was the boy, the messenger sent by the owner, Mr. Braithwaite, who was, of course, white. What else? The smug, contemptuous bitch!

"No," I replied, barely audible with the effort of control. "He did not send it. He brought it."

The sister overheard this little contretemps. She looked at me and raised her shoulders in that familiar slight shrug which told me she understood and sympathized.

Then, to her white colleague she said, "He's Mr. Braithwaite," in quiet tones which did not hide her contempt.

Now should I say to this one beside me, "I am violent, but I know that violence could bring me no real satisfaction. That is my terrible dilemma. When in moments of rage I have felt like abusing someone, or when I have abused someone, it has done nothing to uplift me, to ennoble me, to satisfy me. I may say something as futile as, 'Go to hell, you bastard,' and when I look again you're still there. Your cruelties, your denials, are still there like bars of steel around me. If I thought that through violence I could remove one bar, splinter it into nothingness, I'd pursue violence. If I believed that killing you would free me, I'd kill you. But I know, I surely know that killing you would only increase my helplessness.

"You are a piece of the whole fabric of cruel encagement, and I know inside myself that if I removed you, killed you, millions more like you would spring up like dragon's teeth all around me.

And if everyone like me were to take up arms against you, you'd still proliferate. I live with my rage. But I cannot afford to kill you because of it. Not for you. Never for you. There are times, believe me, there are times when I have wanted to kill. But fortunately or unfortunately the moment passed, forcing me once again to self-examination, and I can see no virtue or value or advantage in such action.

"I am caught between the emotional wish to give violent expression to the rage inside me and a rational appreciation that it would not help me in any way. If I took up arms and shot you, then the police came here and put me away terminally or imprisoned me, so what have I done? How have I helped myself or helped another black man? Or if as I shot you somebody was handy with a gun and shot me, how have I helped myself or how have I helped other black men? Why should we make useless sacrifices of ourselves? If I with a number of blacks; if ten of us blacks killed a hundred whites, it wouldn't make a dent in the white oppressive forces and it would only enrage them even further. How would it help me or other blacks? Perhaps I might temporarily acquire some aura of martyrdom, myself and the other ten. So for today and tomorrow we are martyrs. But even while we are martyrs blacks are hungry, and blacks are without work, and blacks are without consideration and they're mistreated and encaged. And can any black man take real comfort from the fact that I killed ten white men? Emotionally, yes. But how does this assuage his hunger? And how does this fortify him against the cold? Or how does this provide my children or his children with hope and encouragement in their struggle to survive?"

But why bother to say any of it to him? He could never feel the things I feel. Could never begin to understand their deep importance to me. He might ask his questions either from the top of his head or from wherever he claimed his so-called social conscious-ness resides, but he'd never hear my answers. The words, yes. But never the meaning. Because he's white, and in the fact of the color of our skins lies the depth and width of the gulf between us. Let him ask his simple-sounding questions about violence. It's all part of his game. The white man's game. The violence game which the white man wants the black man to play because he knows the black man will lose. Must lose. The dice are not merely loaded against him, offering an unfair bias towards losing, they've been designed specifically to make him a loser. He has no chance. The white man wins and must win because he's numerically superior. He's better equipped with violent ways and means. He's far more expert in the technical and historical application of violence. Coldly, clini-cally expert. In spite of my rage and because of my impotence I must avoid the violence game. I must deny him the satisfaction of inveigling me into those threateningly defensive situations which provide him with the excuse for dispersing, imprisoning or killing me. Us.

There he sat beside me, casually asking his insipid questions about violence. Who was it said that actions speak louder than words? Supposing, just supposing I gave him a practical answer, demonstrating beyond words the thing which right now was eat-ing away at my entrails? What if I stood up, took this question-ing neighbor by his carefully matched shirt and tie and smashed my fist against his smooth-shaven, composed face? Not with any malicious intent. Hell, no! Just to punctuate one philosophical discussion with an illustration of simple, earthy violence. Let him feel the thing he was asking about, so he could decide for himself. Christ! Wouldn't that be something! One, just one solid fist in that well-arranged face would dispel his doubts and answer all his questions at once and forever. More than that, it certainly would wake things up.

What would he do? Yell for help from his fellows? Shout that I'd gone mad? Would he remember that he'd asked me if I was violent? Could he ever accept that that was merely my way of answering him? Never. Anyway. What would such action prove, to him or to myself? He could casually discuss violence as if it were a ball game on the television screen and he was safely on the outside looking in. For me and others like me, violence is a state into which we are born and to which we are conditioned through the hours and days and months and years of painful survival. Could I ever explain to him that nonviolence is nothing but the debasing stamp of the abnormality of our lives? Our human spirits dictate that we be proud and noble. The conditions into which we are forced and pressured economically and socially are violent conditions. Should I enumerate and label them for him? Should I describe for him the corrosive violence of injustice, the rabid violence of hunger, the erosive violence of disease, the debilitating violence of ignorance, the demoralizing violence of unemployment? Or would that be too philosophical for him? Maybe I should remind him of the slaver's whip, the lyncher's rope, the Klansman's blazing torch, the rapings, the shootings, all the myriad expressions of the white man's contempt. All violent.

It is normal to respond violently to oppression. Nations have been born through violent resistance to oppression. It is despicable and abnormal to be submissive in the face of oppression. It is abnormal to be submissive in the face of pressures violently conceived and violently executed. Pressured as I am, human as I am, nonviolence is for me an abnormality. In my weakness I recognize my abnormality, so I sit quietly beside this neighbor, with my violent thoughts controlled to civility, and my violent hands clasped nonviolently in my lap.

"Surely an intelligent man like you knows what his own philosophy is." His voice quite edgy, intruding.

"I know what my personal philosophy is. And it is personal." I see.

"Good. What about your personal philosophy? Is it violent?"

"Personally? No. I don't feel threatened in any way."

"Lucky for you."

"Why? Do you feel threatened?"

"Every black feels threatened by everything around him. What we cannot control threatens us and we control nothing."

"Isn't that a roundabout way of answering my earlier question? If you feel threatened you're likely to be violent. And you say everything threatens you."

"Don't try to put words into my mouth. My answer to you stands, and I still say that we are threatened by everything around us." Keeping it conversationally cool.

"Are you sure you don't hate us?" Leaning forward, the smile anchored in place, the voice cool and level, making light of the question. As if he couldn't care less whether I hated him or not. Them. In answering him I realized I was answering myself. Talking more to myself than to him.

"No. I do not hate you." Smiling as he was smiling. On the outside. "Maybe that's what you would wish me to do. But I've given up on hate. The thing I feel most is rage. Rage, yes, at myself in my helplessness. Rage, yes, to goad myself out of occasions of despair, lest I see you for more than you are, a mere man. But hate, no. I cannot afford to hate you, because in hating you I would only succeed in further impoverishing myself without really hurting you. Long ago during my life in England I learned that you don't really care about my hate because you look through it to my helplessness. You completely ignore my hate. Furthermore, I believe you would not hesitate to encourage my hate in order to continue my helplessness." It was a strain talking to him. Perspiration was trickling down my armpits. "Perhaps you're the one who hates. But I'm not sure even about that. You're contemptuous of me, intolerant of me, but I'm not sure that you hate me. When you have lynched me in a hundred different ways, you've done it casually, contemptuously, secure in your position. Wherever I look I see your contempt. Even when you're being liberal, your contempt comes shining through. You need me helpless so that you can be helpful. You need me violent, hateful and dependent so you can determine and direct my life. The moment I show any sign of thinking for myself, acting for myself, your liberalism is likely to evaporate. Like the ghost that it is."

I felt quite at ease, as if I'd known these things a long, long time, but vaguely, until his questions had brought them finally into focus for me. Meaningful focus.

"Now who's being contemptuous?" he asked. "Who's sneering? You make the word 'liberal' sound dirty, shameful. Should I feel guilty of holding liberal views? Would you deny the generous help liberals have given colored people, and the support liberals have contributed to progressive laws and legislation favorable to Negro progress?" A little heated. Just a trifle I was getting under his skin for a change. Funny, he couldn't quite decide between blacks, Negroes and colored. He used them all.

"I do not impugn liberalism, and my remark was not directed at you, personally. We're being general, aren't we? I am very much in favor of liberals. We're having a liberal conversation. Well, halfway, because in this society the liberal is white. Blacks are militant or extreme or moderate, or subservient Uncle Toms. But never liberal. So, even if only that I might understand the liberal and his viewpoint, I need you. Stay close so I can learn about you. From you."

"Do you really feel that way? Exactly as you state it?" he asked.

"Exactly as I state it."

"You know something? I'm sure that if I had expressed the same sentiment to you about blacks, you'd see me as a racist. In yourself you call it rage. From me you'd call it racism, wouldn't you?"

"Perhaps."

"Then why all the double-talk? If you hate whites, why not be honest and say so?" I could feel the anger in him. It was there, in the tight jaw, in the voice, in the fingers gripping the thin wire shank of his spectacles.

"Because I don't hate you. Not any more. I told you. I cannot afford it. My rage is at myself. If the day ever comes when I'm no longer helpless, I may get around to hating you. Maybe."

"Hate. Rage. It's the same. I can see no difference."

"Can't you? That's a pity. Anyway, there it is. In spite of all you've done to us we have not yet learned to hate you. Not collectively. Sometimes some of us talk of hatred, but that's merely rhetoric because even at such times we talk to you. If we really hated you, we'd have nothing to say to you. Absolutely nothing. Carmichael. Rap Brown. Cleaver. Malcolm X. Jackson. All the brothers spent a lot of time and energy talking to you. Belafonte, Martin Luther King, Ossie Davis, each in his own way talked to you. Have you noticed that even when we erupt into violence we suffer the greatest harm from ourselves? We burn our own homes, destroy our own property, lose our own lives. Whenever the count is taken after every explosive outburst we're the ones who have died or are injured or imprisoned. Watts. Chattanooga. Cincinnati. Harlem. Brooklyn. Newark. Haven't you noticed? If hate were the motivation it would seem that we hate only ourselves. Not you."

"I don't see your point."

"I know you don't. To date we've always been the victims of our own rage. Not hate. Rage. If it were truly hate we'd have long ago localized a target for its release, and you'd be the logical selection. And believe me, we'd have got through to you. You know, I am encouraged to believe that at long last we are learning."

"Learning what? To hate?" He sounded like a bloody broken record.

"No. We're learning to examine the way we feel and the ways in which we react to what we feel. We're learning that the same emotion which caused us to burn and destroy can be re-examined and perhaps channeled to help us build and create. It is one of the main challenges we must face, how to make whatever we are and have work for us. We have been spending far too much time and energy in too many negative pursuits, the worst of which has been crying about our pain. To you. We've been so blind in our helplessness that we look to you for help. Isn't that the quintessence of irony? Your contempt for us is basic to our many problems, yet we expect you to help us resolve those problems. It's like asking the criminal to be at the same time judge and jury. Our preoccupation should be educating ourselves, teaching ourselves to be thoughtful, resourceful men. Men with pride in ourselves. Acutely conscious of our dignity. We need to believe, in ourselves. In that way we can perhaps escape the tyranny of our weakness and your exploitation of it."

"Does this mean separation? When you say you'll educate your-selves, do you mean separately from whites?"

"No. I thought I'd already answered that. I'm not talking about separate institutions. I'm talking about a new appreciation of ourselves, expressed among us, understood by us, believed by us, inculcated in our children. An appreciation of our worth and our ability to direct and exploit that worth to our advantage. This would mean taking our eyes off you and focusing them beyond you. Towards infinity, so that we remove the limits, the ceilings you have placed on our endeavors, our potential. That's why we can't afford to hate you. It would mean making you the focus of our interests and you're really not worth it."

The red appeared around his neck, moving quickly upward. I went on, "We've got to learn to feel pride in ourselves. Real pride in being black men. And women. A pride which springs naturally from an appreciation of our worth. We've got to learn to live above the myths you've created and fostered in us about us. The myth about our intellectual inferiority. The myth of our dependence on you."

He leaned backward as if for greater comfort, tilting his head upward to look beyond me towards the grimy window. There was silence between us. This is it, I thought. We've said it all and are back where we began, distant as ever. All the talking had done nothing for us. Hell. I didn't even know his name.

The train had stopped, but there was no movement among the passengers towards the exits. I leaned forward to peer through the window, but could see only an unbroken line of grimy buildings. The conductor pushed himself along the aisle with an occasional "'Scuse me, please. 'Scuse me." Always just out of reach of ques-tions about the unscheduled stop. Murmurs of irritation. Specula-tion about the cause of delay.

"Tell me. Are you a churchman? I mean, are you religious?" my neighbor asked. Suddenly. Taking me completely by surprise. I was amazed at his persistence, at his unshatterable gall. With so much aplomb he should wind up as president. At least. What was it with him? Maybe he was determined to prove how bloody civilized he was.

"No. I'm not religious. But why do you ask?"

"Just something about the things you've been saying. Something about you . . . "

Why did memory so readily revive pictures of me, perhaps four or five years old, kneeling beside my bed and repeating the prayers on which my mother insisted as part of the bedtime ritual. " . . . and please bless Gram and Grandpa and Tantie Alma and Daddy and Mum. And please bless me." Her strong warm hug and smiling kiss my reward for saying it correctly. Growing up. Able to repeat,

> *Now I lay me down to sleep*
> *I pray the Lord my soul to keep.*
> *If I should die before I wake*
> *I pray the Lord my soul to take.*

Somewhat frightened by the words "die" and "soul to take," but reassured by my mother's powerful presence near by. Too young to understand the meaning of death. Then one day my father was unwell. The next day he was taken away to the hospital. I never saw him again. My mother explained that he had gone away to be with the angels. Sometimes, at night, I'd lie in my bed and look out through the window at the Guyana sky, black and heavy with stars, seeming close enough for me to reach upward and touch them. I'd imagine my father somewhere up there, able to move about as he wished, even without wings. A little hurt that he did not come down to see me and talk with me, but understanding that it was perhaps too far away.

Later occasions when, in despair over my difficulties with a Latin or Greek assignment, or sweating through riders on a geometric theorem, I'd whisper the request "Please, God, help me," sometimes even audibly. Doubling and redoubling the effort, then telling myself that the successful outcome was due to the prayer. Not quite believing it, but never quite doubting it either, just in case I'd need to do it again. And again.

That day in 1943, returning to base, after a simple "recce" practice flight, to find the airfield covered in thick ground mists which had drifted or been blown over from near-by low-lying fenlands. The voice of Operations Control quietly encouraging. Checking my instruments. Not enough fuel for diversion elsewhere. Listening to that voice and its directions, carefully making my circuit to line up for approach. Depth perception distorted by the thick, swirling mists. Feeling the way down in a gentle glide, stick and rudder bars like extensions of myself, the altimeter my crystal ball of truth. Watching it inch away the feet. Prayer words in my mind, whispering them desperately to the God in whom my mother believed. The airplane a living, breathing thing, reaching blindly downward for its roost.

Suddenly breaking through the mist, the runway directly ahead and little more than two hundred feet below. I'd made it. Shouting the words into the open-channel circuit, operations agreeing. Readily forgetting the unspoken promises of piety or penance.

Religious? Hardly. Those weeks and months of job hunting. Embittered by rejection and my own helplessness against it. Passing a church early one morning, the side door open. Slipping in. Quietly alone in that towering, cold emptiness. The sun barely filtering through the orderly patterns of colored glass to break the heavy gloom. Self-consciously kneeling. Whispering my request for help in finding a job. Any job. Hearing nothing. Feeling nothing. Finally sitting up, disgusted with myself for being there and going through a tiresome rigmarole in which I did not believe. And yet, at the same time, wishing for the impossible miracle.

Thinking, as if in mockery of myself, as if prompted by an adversary voice in my ear, "God created man in His own image. In the image of God, created He man." I must have learned that at Sunday school. With all the other texts. God is love. Remembered now, when I found the face of man turned contemptuously from me, and the blending of God with man quite unbearable. "In His own image," the text had said. God and me. Me and God. Okay. Then why the hell couldn't all those white bastards see that? Why couldn't they recognize His image in me? Why was I being forced to crawl to them, God-me begging the crust to fill my Divine stomach?

I was forgetting. Oh Christ! I was forgetting. Up there in those windows, among the pieces of green and purple and blue and gold, red and yellow, among the black strips of sealing lead, the faces were all pinky white. On the illustrated text cards they'd given me at Sunday school, the faces had all been pinky white. Angels. Disciples. Mary. All of them. Christ, too. Bearded, slim and withdrawn, with upcast eyes. But white. And God. How had He been depicted? Faceless. Bodiless. Always a symbol. A huge all-seeing Eye. A flaming sword. A burning bush.

Yes. That was it. The representations and the symbols had all been white. So why the hell was I wasting my time? Getting up and striding out, the steel tips on my heels ringing my aggressive despair on the intricately tiled floor.

And the next time. Michelle, my beloved. Lovely and intelligent beyond her nine years, suddenly stricken and dying of an incurable illness. Again I prayed to God, to all the gods, out of a desperate need I had not imagined possible. Begging their collective pity. Desperately, sincerely, offering myself on whatever altar they might choose, only that she should live. Watching the light gradually fade from her pain-filled eyes. Mute to her barely audible question, "Will I get well and go home with you, Daddy?" The last vestige of my belief slipping away into the void with her final breath.

He was quite extraordinary, this neighbor of mine. I'd really believed that we'd said the final words to each other, but he'd opened it again. This time he'd switched to religion. Maybe he was merely being friendly and seeking ways of showing it. Perhaps, in spite of his so-called black friends and business associates, being in this captive situation with me confused him. Anyway, a friendly gesture is a friendly gesture. The least I could do was meet him halfway. It was really no strain. I'd had plenty of experience in the techniques of observing the social civilities.

"What about you?" I asked him. "Are you religious?"

"Yes. I consider myself a religious man," he replied.

"A churchman?" I was simply feeding him his own cues. For civility's sake.

"Yes. My family has attended the same church for generations."

He said it with a certain pride, continuing with, "Nowadays religion is considered old-fashioned. My own children are much less interested in going to church than I was at their age. In the final analysis we all need something to believe in, to give us spiritual anchorage." Pausing, looking at me as if expecting either confirmation or denial. Nothing from me.

"I believe that God is the divine architect and director of man's destiny," he went on. "I believe in truth and justice and the responsibility for dealing fairly with my fellow man."

Still nothing from me. I wondered why he felt compelled to talk. I didn't give a damn what he believed or did not believe. The words were coming out of him like water from a tap, without any hint of conviction. I wondered what he meant by the words "truth" and "justice" and "fellow man." They fell from his lips as casually as "fairly" and "destiny." Just words. Was I included among his "fellow man"?

"I know you said you're not religious," he said. "Perhaps we're not using the same terms for the same things, but I'm sure that a man like you must believe in something."

"I do." I told him.

"Good." Leaning closer. "What is it? Can you talk about it?"

"Certainly. I believe in challenge." Saying it to him as the thought coalesced in my mind. Surprising myself with the sudden recognition of it. Hearing the words of the idea I'd been struggling with these many years. At last it had surfaced, bursting out from its hiding place, teased into the open by persistent pressure from this neighbor. I'd finally confronted myself with it. The look on his face told me he did not understand.

"Challenge?" He removed the spectacles to peer nearsightedly at me. The quiver of little muscles around his mouth signaled the beginning of a smile.

"Yes. Challenge."

"I'm afraid I don't understand."

"Perhaps it's more important for me fully to understand it myself than attempt to explain it to you. In any case I don't believe that explaining it to you would serve any purpose. However, I'll tell you this much. All around me there are influences which seek to reduce me, limit me or obstruct me. You are part of those influences. Wherever I look I am confronted with proscriptions designed and maintained by you. For much of my life I struck out blindly at them, threatened by them, frightened of them. At last, perhaps a bit late, I'm seeing the challenge implicit in them. I see each of them, wherever or whenever it occurs, as a challenge to myself, to my right to be fully myself, to realize my full potential. I am no longer frightened. I accept the challenge."

"I still don't get it," he said, moving his head negatively to reinforce the words.

"That does not surprise me." I replied, then thought I'd pull the issue a little closer around him. "Wouldn't you agree that six feet one inch of intelligent humanity should be a truly considerable force? That's how I see myself, and the sight of you challenges me to be exactly that. A considerable force, determined to occupy every inch of physical and spiritual space my stature requires. Every kind of contact with you reaffirms that challenge. Day in, day out."

"Are you saying that just being here, talking like this, is a challenge to you?" Asking the question in a tone of voice which implied that the idea was incredible to him.

"Sure. Your presence beside me challenges me to project my humanity. You took that seat reluctantly because you are conditioned to think of me as less than human. My natural inclination is to avoid contact with you, even conversational contact, because you wear the whole history of your attitude to me. But now I see you in that history and I am challenged to acknowledge your presence, talk with you, be courteous to you, as a man. See what I mean?"

The spectacles were back in place, the face still inclined to me. I felt the gaze but could not see the eyes. Silence from him.

Perhaps I'd wasted my time talking to him that way, saying all that to him. Could he just now overcome his conditioned way of seeing me to really hear what I was saying? Not bloody likely! I could never explain to him the unnaturalness of being challenged spiritually to respond to the most natural of human needs, the most ordinary of human conditions? I'd mentioned courtesy, but what of the other wider, deeper areas of human relationship? Friendship. Love. Would he ever be able to understand what it means to be challenged to respond to friendship readily, spontaneously offered against the ubiquitous historical backdrop of racial mistrust? And what about love? This one had circuitously inquired at "deeper relationships" in Paris. He'd never dare ask about "deeper relationships" in New Canaan. We'd never dare talk about love. Not him and me.

For me, to me, the word had become bigger than him and his whiteness and me and my blackness. Every day it stared me in the face, prodding me to live up to its challenges. As it had done for the past twenty years, ever since that evening when my first class graduated.

For nine months I'd worked with them, swinging hourly like a pendulum between hope and despair. At myself. At them. For most of those nine months I was so preoccupied with trying to teach them, as pupils, that I very nearly missed the opportunity of seeing them as persons. Even when, belatedly, I discovered them behind and beneath the superficialities of the way they dressed, spoke and deported themselves, my concern was for myself. Find out about them the better to teach them. That was the strategy.

In the last hour of the last day we spent together they made me a gift. On the container box they'd written: "To Sir, With Love."

In the instant of reading it I'd learned another lesson. In using the word "love" they'd declared themselves to me. So easily they could have used words like "respect" and "affection." Either of those would have been right considering the early nature and difficult progress of our relationship. But they'd used the word "love." They'd handed it to me with their gift, meaning every letter of it, and had then gone their separate ways, leaving it to haunt the rest of my life with its challenge. Its challenge to growth; its challenge to stature; its challenge to live.

Suddenly remembering that day, December 28, 1971. Still shaken up from a recent bout of flu in London, and waiting at Heathrow Airport for my plane to Paris. Sitting in the airport lounge, trying to select the flight announcements from the general hubbub of multilingual conversations and the rise and fall of engine noise from the crowded tarmac. Two small children, a boy and a girl, dressed so alike they may have been twins, chased each other in a noisily, endless game of hide-and-seek, darting among the passengers and their baggage. Now and then they'd return, breathless, to an attractive blonde woman who'd hug them absentmindedly then quickly disengage themselves to continue their game. The girl was the leader, imperiously dictating each venture to her sturdier but compliant playmate. They were an attractive couple in their red woolen ski suits and sealskin ankle boots. The boy's hair was close cropped, the girl's a shoulder-length mass of blonde curls. Finns or Icelanders, I guessed.

Their play eventually brought them racing along near where I sat, the boy ahead. His sister caught sight of me, stopped and came to me, a look of wonder on her face. Unhesitating, she came near and touched both sides of my face with her hands, looked at her fingers, laughed delightedly, then threw her arms about my neck and kissed me. Releasing me, she said some words which were quite unintelligible to me and, laughing, hurried off in pursuit of her brother. The wonderful innocence of it. She saw the difference between us, wondered at it, accepted it.

How could I explain any of that to this man beside me?

"It seems to me," he was speaking again, spacing each word separately from the other, perhaps for effect, "that anyone who considers it a challenge to engage in an ordinary conversation like this must have a lot of hatred locked up inside him." Looking away, as if the words were enough to damn me forevermore. They didn't bother me, not one little bit.

"I told you before," I answered. "The word is rage, not hatred. Anyway, even hating you would be no problem for me. No problem at all. Everything around me easily encourages it. The trick is to try the opposite thing." Whether he believed me or not was of little consequence.

"And the opposite thing is loving." Investing each word with his cynical disbelief.

"I need something big enough to counterbalance my racist feelings." I threw it at him. The gray eyes bulged perceptibly.

"Are you now saying that you're *a* racist? Advertising it?" I'm sure his voice was up an octave.

"Not *a* racist. Just racist. I'm racist. You're racist. We're all racist. All of us. Every bloody member of this racist society."

"I'd suggest that you speak for yourself. Not for me. I'm certainly not a racist."

191

"Good for you. It takes some doing to be the only one in step while everyone else is stumbling around. In Guyana we have a saying, 'If you attend the crabs' dance you must get muddy.' We live in a racist society. We work, eat, sleep, fornicate, are born and die in a racist environment. Differences are more important to us than similarities. Those differences govern our lives. All our lives. The most obvious ones, the most exploited and exploitable ones, are race and color." The telltale red appeared at his neck, spreading irregularly upward. The smile was gone. In its place a look of shock. Anger. His mouth opened once or twice, then closed tight, the area around his lips turning white under the pressure. I felt quite calm.

"The single fact of color or race is the most divisive element in many societies. Including this one. Too black to attend this school. Too black to live in this neighborhood. Too black to swim on this beach. Too black to run for high political office. Too black to be buried in this piece of earth. We're all involved in it. All of us. Those who aggressively pursue racist policies. Those who are victimized by those policies. Those who are in-between, like Minnehaha, neither willing nor reluctant. We're all racist."

"That's your opinion, and you're welcome to it." He finally got the words out. "I concede that in this country we have many problems but that does not make us all raving racists." Even now, in spite of the anger still shining in his eyes, the words came out without much heat.

"I didn't use the word 'raving,' but perhaps it's very apropos. I watched the television coverage of things like the Selma march, the Watts riots, the pickets at Pontiac, Michigan and Forest Hills, New York. Did you look at the faces of the men and women as they screamed their threats and abuse? Black faces. White faces. All contorted with fury and anger. Unreason. Yes, I think the term 'raving' would have been just right. And the other things. Bombing of school buses. Burning of occupied homes while the families are asleep. Bombing churches while children sat in Sunday school worshipping your familiar God. Who but raving lunatics would do such things?"

"Those are extreme cases," he managed.

"Are they? Then would you say that those angry pickets at Forest Hills are extremists? No, my friend. Sometimes the cameras would focus on a face twisted in passionate anger, like a fury from hell. A few moments later I'd notice that face again, the anger less rabid, belonging to an ordinary body in ordinary clothes. Tall, short, slim, fat, handsome or homely. But ordinary. That's the sobering part. They are all so bloody ordinary. As I am. As you are."

"The people of Forest Hills are mainly Jewish," he said, reprovingly.

"Are they? So racism is no respecter of persons or religions. Do you know what I did last Sunday?" He'd been asking all the questions until now, or nearly all. Now it was my turn.

"I'm listening," he replied.

"I drove up Park Street to the Shell gas station, left my car to be filled and serviced, and walked behind the station to look at the church, that beautifully white structure with its tall finger probing the clouds. I watched the people arriving, parking their cars, chatting with each other and going inside. Ordinary people. No doubt very nice people. Models of suburban respectability. Perhaps comfortably off. Easily fitting the mould of the decent, law-abiding, hard-working, God-fearing citizen. The salt of the earth. And sane. I closed my eyes for a moment and the transition was easy. Forest Hills to New Canaan. New Canaan to Forest Hills."

"I doubt that you'd see pickets out in New Canaan." So cool. We could have been talking of the recent snowfall.

"I agree. Zoning laws and all that."

"Well, did you get some satisfaction from watching them go to church?"

"Oh, I wasn't looking for satisfaction. Looking at them was like looking at myself and understanding that I, too, was easily capable of the same raving, lunatic, racist behavior."

"I'm quite sure that everyone in Forest Hills was not on the picket lines. Some people up there do not oppose the project, but I don't suppose that the liberal point of view interests you. No doubt liberals are included in your collective of racists."

"Of course. As I see it, a liberal is someone consciously struggling with his own racism. Just as I'm struggling with mine. The label does not mean a damn thing."

"And you say you believe in love."

"I said I believe in challenge." Keeping him in line.

After a pause he asked me, "Why did you decide to leave New York to live in New Canaan? I would have thought that the city would provide you with everything you needed." He was quite at ease.

"Not quite everything. I moved because I'm an addict."

His head jerked around at the word, his eyes swiveling uneasily. "An addict?"

"Yes. I'm hooked on clean air and open spaces and lots of growing green." The relief on his face was funny to watch.

"Oh, I see. Tell me. What's your opinion of our local community? I take it you've lived there long enough to have an opinion?"

Did I detect a note of sarcasm? "It's a very pleasant community," I told him.

"You really mean that?"

"Yes."

"Are you sure?"

I made no further reply, waiting for him to show me where it was leading.

"I take it then that nobody demonstrated against your presence in the town or attempted to burn your home." Really enjoying himself. Good. I'd even help him.

"No. Not a single picket. Not a single match."

"And you still say we're racist?"

"That's right. New Canaan is a piece of the whole, as is Watts and Selma, and Pontiac and Forest Hills."

"But you've never been molested. You're free to come and go as you please." He was funny. Pitifully funny. Using the word "free" but evidently having no idea of its real import. I could feel the rage quickly ballooning. He was so aggressively defensive when I'd said this society is racist, yet here he was, expecting me to do somersaults because I could sleep peaceably in my bed and walk unmolested in the street. Damn it! It was not something which he'd conferred on me by his grace and favor.

I realized that the word which so easily stirred me really meant nothing to him. He'd never had to think of freedom, for himself. He really knew nothing of the condition of freedom, or the components of that condition. To him it was, "You're free to come and go." Come where? Go where? What the hell did he know of freedom? He'd never had his right to it questioned, never felt that his entitlement to it was threatened in any way. What the hell did he know of being free to come and go? I thought of my recent visit to Atlanta, Georgia. From the airport to the hotel the taxi driver had maintained a running commentary on the city, pinpointing for my benefit the highlights of redesign along Peachtree Avenue.

Approaching the hotel, he said, "Time was when none of us could go in there, man." He was black.

After registering, I inquired at the desk about restaurants in the vicinity and was told of an excellent one near by, locally famous for its grilled steaks. After a shower, shave and change of clothes I went there. A hostess courteously greeted me at the door and showed me to a seat. The decor was pleasing, the room spacious, each table with its burden of spotless napery and gleaming cutlery. The uniformed help all smartly elegant. All white. Remembering the words of the taxi driver, I reminded myself that I was in Atlanta, Georgia. In the Southland. Free to enter that restaurant, free to sit and be served. I ordered an *apéritif*, then my meal, helpfully advised by the waiter on the specialties of the house. I sipped my drink while waiting, thinking about the South and the little of its history I had read. Yes, only yesterday I would not have been allowed in. Today I was able to buy accommodation at the best hotel in town or a meal in the finest restaurant. If this was freedom it had been dearly bought with the blood of many, black like me, who, not so long ago, had sought for none of these frills. All they had demanded was the right to live like men. Free in body, in mind and spirit. Not merely to come and go. Any disconnected soul can do that. But free to be a part of everything around them. Free to contribute, out of the fullness of their potential, to the growth, the development, the stature, the pride, the strength, the power, to everything which made their country live and thrive. For that they had reached. For that they had died. They had rejected both the fact and the spirit of slavery, and for that they had been brutalized, shot, lynched and imprisoned by those who casually accepted the notion and fact of their own freedom as inalienable.

Now here I was, an extension of all those who, black like me, had ever passed this way. For them there had been no room at inn or lunch counter. Instead of courteous service they'd received clubs and curses. Try as I might, I could not tear my mind away from the recent historic past and the wavering images it conjured up. Freedom must mean more than this.

The meal was placed before me. Considering the astounding collective cost, it was, surprisingly, only food, invested with no special virtue. The few dollars listed on the menu seemed but a minute fraction of the whole terrible price. I could not eat it. I put enough money on the table for the food, drink and tip and left.

The train slowed and stopped. We were in Grand Central Station.

By the time I reached down my briefcase from the rack he'd stepped into the aisle. Someone moved in behind him in the hurried procession out on to the platform. My companion did not look back. In the crowd he was soon lost to view.

About the Author

E. R. Braithwaite was born in British Guiana (now Guyana) in 1912. Educated at the City College of New York and the University of Cambridge, he served in the Royal Air Force during World War II. Braithwaite spent 1950 to 1960 in London, first as a schoolteacher and then as a welfare worker—experiences he describes in *To Sir, With Love* and *Paid Servant*, respectively. In 1966 he was appointed Guyana's ambassador and permanent representative to the United Nations. He has also held positions at the World Veterans Federation and UNESCO, was a professor of English at New York University's Institute for Afro-American Affairs, and taught creative writing at Howard University. The author of five nonfiction books and two novels, he currently lives in Washington, DC.

OPEN ROAD
INTEGRATED MEDIA

Open Road Integrated Media is a digital publisher and multimedia content company. Open Road creates connections between authors and their audiences by marketing its ebooks through a new proprietary online platform, which uses premium video content and social media.

CPSIA information can be obtained
at www.ICGtesting.com
Printed in the USA
FSHW021956271019
63464FS